Other books by Richard and/or Linda Eyre*

Lifebalance
Teaching Your Children Values
Three Steps to a Strong Family
I Didn't Plan to Be a Witch
The Awakening (a novel)
What Manner of Man
Teaching Your Children Responsibility
Teaching Your Children Sensitivity
Teaching Your Children Joy
Don't Just Do Something, Sit There
The Wrappings and the Gifts
Children's Stories to Teach Joy
Stewardship of the Heart

*If you have difficulty locating any title, call (801) 581-0112 or (800) 772-4859 to order direct.

spiritual

Serendipity

Cultivating and Celebrating
the Art of the Unexpected

RICHARD EYRE
SIMON & SCHUSTER

SIMON & SCHUSTER
Rockefeller Center
1230 Avenue of the Americas
New York, NY 10020

Designed by Bonni Leon-Berman

Manufactured in the United States of America

1   3   5   7   9   10   8   6   4   2

Library of Congress Cataloging-in-Publication Data
Eyre, Richard M.
Spiritual serendipity : cultivating and celebrating the art
of the unexpected / Richard Eyre.
p.   cm.
Includes bibliographical references and index.
1. Spiritual life.   2. Serendipity.   I. Title.
BL624.E97   1997
291.4'4—dc21   96-40114
CIP

ISBN 0-684-80786-6

"serendipity"

Popular definition: A happy accident.

Webster definition: The making of pleasant discoveries by accident, the knack of doing this.

Original definition: The quality or faculty, through awareness and good fortune, of being able to find something good while seeking something else.

Spiritual serendipity: The same quality, but with the added input and direction of spiritual receptivity and divine guidance.

contents

The Land of Serendip

As I write, I'm sitting on the veranda of my room in Sri Lanka, looking out through the jungle toward the beach, watching a man lead his elephant into the sea for a bath. Perhaps it is a rather extreme approach, but I've come here, halfway around the world, to a teardrop-shaped island in the Indian Ocean, to explore the origins and the deeper meanings of my favorite word, *serendipity*, and to write a book I hope will share the power of these meanings with others.

Serendipity, a word coined by an eighteenth-century British writer named Horace Walpole, suggests an attitude of mind and heart that can give people the means to move from where they are to where they want to be, and perhaps even from where they are to where God wants them to be.

I came to Sri Lanka, which was once called Serendip, because I thought the book ought to carry part of the mystery of this ancient land and of the legend that spawned the word. I will begin, after this brief foreword, by telling you how and why Walpole created the word and about an old Persian fable called "The Three Princes of Serendip" that inspired him. I found the fable, one of the few copies of it left in the world, in the British Museum in London, and retranslated it into modern English. But before we get into that, let me make a comment, based in part on the perspective I feel as I look at *our* world from this faraway place.

Americans, as the world starts not only a new century but a new millennium, live in a unique society and culture that is more challenging, more complex, and more competitive than any other. Compared to people of other places and other times, our lives are bountiful as well as busy, but they are almost always demanding and almost never predictable. No matter what course we choose, life is filled with surprises and unexpected turns in the road

The stress and frustration that most of us feel traces back both to the demands and to the unpredictability. Over and over, it seems, just as we begin to get an idea of where we're going or what we're doing, something comes along— a crisis, a challenge, a circumstance—and suddenly we're in uncharted waters (and over our heads).

The problems we face are too diverse to have

a single answer—unless that answer is an *attitude:* an attitude that can give guidance to life, an attitude that can turn adversity into advantage, impatience into insight, competition into charity, boredom into beauty—an attitude or a paradigm called *spiritual serendipity.*

In a way this trip to Serendip symbolizes the core idea of this book. I came here because I felt guided to or prompted to. It wasn't a particularly logical decision, or a financially justifiable one. And it's not a very planned trip because I don't know the options or what to expect. It is so much easier (and perceived as more desirable) to do things for more practical reasons—and to be in control, in charge, to plan and manage and even manipulate. We like to say, "act, don't react" or "have plans and contingency plans" or "leave nothing to chance" or "never be surprised."

But the fact is that we know so little and control so little. Surprises happen every day. And there are so many big things and so many small things over which we have no control.

The fact is that, on our own, we don't know enough about the future, or about those around us, or even about ourselves to choose very consistently what is best for ourselves and best for others.

But there is a higher intelligence which can prompt and guide our minds and spirits with small, sometimes hard-to-notice feelings and insights that we call nudges or impressions or intuitions or inspirations. *Spiritual Serendipity* is an attitude that increases our receptivity to this purer intelligence. With it, we can discard the futile goal of a totally self-managed life and adopt the goal of a *guided* life. May I find more of it (and share more of it with you) while I am here.

 Richard Eyre
*Sri Lanka (formerly
Ceylon and before that
Serendip)
Off the south coast of
India
Very late in the
twentieth century*

A Word from Linda Eyre

My husband, Richard, you need to understand, is intrigued by somewhat weird, rather obscure *words*. I told him that "serendipity" sounded more like a band or a singing group than a book—and "spiritual serendipity" sounded like a tongue twister or maybe a gospel singing group.

I told him he ought to call the book *Receptivity to Intuition or Inspiration* because that's really what it is about. Or, if he insists on alliteration, how about *Gaining Guidance* or *Discovering and Discerning Deep or Divine Direction*.

Actually, Richard's fascination with serendipity began before and during our courtship and was so intense by the time we had our first baby that he wanted to call her Serendipity. I dissuaded him with my observation that kids might call her Dipity. Still, the best I could get was a compromise and we named her Saren. Except that everyone calls her Sara or Sharon, I guess that has worked out fine (though it is a little embarrassing when people say, "What does that name mean?" and we have to say, "A happy accident"). Someone sent a baby gift that was an embroidered blanket labeled Saren Wrap. I'm just glad our first child wasn't a boy, or Richard would have wanted to name him after the English author who invented the word serendipity: *Horace* Walpole.

Seriously, though, bear with Richard and his strange terminology. I've come to appreciate the word almost as much as he does. It means, at least in this book, a lot of powerful things and it stands for a truly revolutionary new way of living (and a new way of thinking) that increases our *joy* as well as our effectiveness.

I think what Richard has done here is to use the "sandwich" format for this book. The beginning and ending of the book are the two slices of bread—they motivate us by making some remarkable promises about what spiritual serendipity can do for those who obtain it. The "meat" in the middle consists of explorations of the serendipity concept and solid suggestions about *how* people can gain the quality, and through it become more receptive, more aware, and much, much happier.

Let me mention Richard's writing style. Sometimes he writes poetry and sometimes he writes prose. And sometimes, as in this book, he writes some of each and mostly something that is a combination of the two. At other times, he tells a story, usually about a personal experience. It's a little different, but rather appropriate in this book, where Richard is *suggesting* ideas and feelings that we have all had before. He is drawing out of our minds things

that we already know but have not yet connected . . . so that we will read a page or two
and say, "Ah ha."

I've enjoyed working with my husband in
writing this book. I recommend it to you, but
then I can't be objective, can I? So read it and
see what you think, or, better put, see if the
book gives you some exciting new *ways* of
thinking for yourself.

Linda J. Eyre
Serendip, Sri Lanka
(You didn't think he
came here without
me, did you?)

o v e r t u r e

Living in a World Being Spiritually Reborn

What's happening?

I go to New York and the number one play and the number one books are about *angels.*

I walk into a bookstore and the best-selling fiction is on quests for meaning and supernatural insights. The best-selling nonfiction is about values, virtues, the spirit and the soul.

I read the national opinion polls, which tell me that more than 60 percent of Americans feel the need to experience spiritual growth.

I go to my publishers who used to urge me to modify or delete any "spirit" or "soul" terminology in my "mainstream" books, and they now tell me to use more of "those words."

I show them a deeply spiritual book that I wrote for family and friends and not for publication, and they say the general market is ready for it.

Here is what I think is happening: We are living in a world that is being spiritually reborn. We want deeper answers, deeper meaning, deeper feelings. We're more interested in finding divine help than in proving we don't need it. We feel less and less external security on our streets and in our society, so we look for internal security in our souls. We haven't found the answers or the peace we want in the material or the "outer," so we're seeking them in the spiritual or the "inner."

What if I told you that, at some point, self-help becomes an oxymoron . . . that ultimately we all need help from a higher source . . . that relying totally on self is more a folly than a virtue . . . that "there is nothing you can't do" is a fallacy, that the truth is, there's nothing we can do—of real worth—without spiritual help?

Would you feel challenged, combative, prone to argue with me? Or would you feel that I was a kindred spirit, that you and I have something in common? Would you hope that perhaps the book you hold in your hands, though you may have found it in the self-help section, may reveal a new level, a new dimension of help?

A New Paradigm for Living

Spiritual Serendipity is the first book in the "paradigm trilogy."* It deals with a new paradigm, a different, more spiritual way of viewing and perceiving the events and people in our everyday lives. It is, after all, how we see things that determines both what and how we *feel* . . . and *do*. It is written from the perspective and conviction that we are spiritual beings and can communicate (both "sending" and "receiving") with a greater spiritual being.

This, of course, is a mainstream perspective. More than 95 percent of Americans profess belief in God or a supreme being and over 90 percent of us believe there is a spirit within ourselves that separates from our bodies at death.

---

*The second book, *Spiritual Stewardship*, probes the error and the inaccuracy of ownership and blames most of the world's prejudice, intolerance, insecurity, and guilt on it. It then calls for a paradigm shift to the more tolerant, more fulfilling, and more accurate notion of stewardship. The final book, *Spiritual Synergy*, suggests that the total can be greater than the sum of its parts in three separable and powerful relationships: body and spirit, husband and wife, and man with God.

Together, the three books of the trilogy take issue with what may be the three most frantic pursuits of our day—the pursuits of control, of ownership, and of independence—suggesting in their place the more spiritual pursuits of serendipity, stewardship, and synergy.

Nevertheless, this book is not directly or definitively about God or the spirit. It is about a paradigm—about perspectives or attitudes that can change (enhance and improve) how we see ourselves, our relationships, and our world. It is about viewing things in an eternal rather than an earthly perspective. And since God and the spirit are *reality*, it is about seeing things more *realistically* and more *accurately*. It is about avoiding the deception and pain of viewing things materialistically, coincidentally, or as though man were in charge.

Judging by much of our current literature and entertainment, spiritual perspectives are popular right now, even trendy. But trying to understand things spiritually (rather than just sensually or scientifically) is far more than a recent trend. For most of mankind's recorded history people looked principally to the spiritual or the mystical for answers and explanations. Only during the relatively brief period of the past few hundred years did society look more to the secular than to the spiritual for understanding. (The corruption of many church and religious institutions in the late Middle Ages and the emergence of early versions of natural science caused people to turn from one to the other for answers and explanations.) And it is the *inadequacy* of secular answers that is now turning us back to more spiritual paradigms. We want knowledge and insight beyond what we can learn through our five senses. We want personal answers to questions that science doesn't even attempt to deal with. We want to understand more than academics or philosophy can tell us, and we want our lives and our destinies to be guided by something wiser and more insightful than ourselves.

The basic premise of this book, and the essence of the paradigm it suggests, is that we simply cannot gain enough data through our senses to consistently make the best decisions for ourselves and those around us—that thinking we can do anything and control everything in our personal life is the highest form of self-deceit. The premise here is that most things, even personal things, are beyond our real control, that relaxing and thinking things through often brings more results than thrashing and forcing, and that there exists a source of far higher intelligence and power that we can tap into. In light of that greater source, the goal of a *guided* life is better than the goal of a self-determined life. The most important claim of this book is that people can *develop an attitude and a state of mind* that makes guidance and spiritual serendipity more likely, more frequent, and far more consequential.

Serendipity

Serendipity is commonly defined as "a happy accident" and takes its name from the island of Sri Lanka, which used to be called Ceylon and, before that, Serendip.

The notion of serendipity—of valuable discoveries made while seeking something else entirely—can be illustrated by experience in almost every field.

In medicine, Sir Alexander Fleming left a window open and the wind blew contaminants onto his staphylococcus culture. Before long, as the contaminating mold grew on his petri dish, Fleming noticed that, near the mold, the colonies of staphylococcus were undergoing dissolution. Fleming (who once said "chance favors the trained mind") observed the phenomenon, isolated the mold in pure culture, and discovered penicillin.

In physics, Wilhelm Roentgen, who was experimenting with electricity and vacuum tubes, noticed the fluorescence of a barium phatinocyanide screen that happened to be lying near. He found that this radiation could pass through substances opaque to ordinary light and affect a photographic plate. The X ray was born.

In chemistry, Charles Goodyear, who had tried for years to take the stickiness out of rubber, one night by chance left a piece of rubber smeared with sulphur near a hot stove and the next morning it was vulcanized.

A music teacher named Robert Fouks, walking home through a dense fog, heard his daughter playing the piano, but only one note came through. He used that one bass note to invent the foghorn.

Robert Watson observed that overhead aircraft gave reflected signals from radio waves and thus he discovered radar.

Phoenician sailors used lumps of saltpeter for their cooking kettles. When they melted and ran over the sand they produced glass.

As valuable as serendipity has been through the ages and in the macro developments of so many fields, it can be *most* valuable now, in the micro developments of our everyday lives.

At the birth of a new millennium we have all kinds of new pressures, new complexities, new challenges. We play the faster game of life by new and sometimes blurred rules. Options, opportunities, and obstacles exist in incredible variety! The old tools of time management and the old approaches of positive mental attitude don't work as well as they used to. Trying to control or manipulate or plan everything just sets us up for frustration. There's too much going on, and unexpected changes come too fast.

We miss too much if all we see is our list. We kid ourselves if we think we know enough to plan everything. To enjoy and succeed in this new world we need right-brain receptiveness as well as left-brain logic. For what's here now, and for what's coming, we need new attitudes, new approaches, and new answers. But the answers we need are not really new. They are as old as time—and scripture:

Go to now, ye that say, Today or tomorrow we will go into such a city, and continue there a year, and buy and sell and get gain:

Whereas ye know not what shall be on the morrow . . .

For what ye ought to say, If the Lord will, we shall live, and do this, or that.

James 4:13–15

As we try to shift from attitudes of control, manipulation, and self-determination to attitudes of awareness and guidance, it helps to have a *name* for our new approach. Horace Walpole gave us a name, or part of one, more than two centuries ago. He read an ancient Persian fable called "The Three Princes of Serendip," which told the story of three brothers whose alertness and sagacity allowed them to consistently *discover things that were far better than what they had been seeking*. Walpole coined

the word "serendipity" and defined it as the gift
or faculty for finding something good while
seeking something else.

Serendipity can be *developed*, as an attitude
of the mind and as a quality of the spirit. It
can energize and excite our lives and give us
balance between structure and spontaneity, between flat, fixed firmness and free, fun flexibility. It can allow us to get there *and* to enjoy the
journey at the same time. It can enable us to
tap into a higher, clearer kind of reality and in-
ject joy into what is no longer routine.

And for those who believe in God, serendipity of the spirit can be an attitude whereby our
lives become divinely guided rather than self-
structured. Serendipity of the spirit can become the connecting bridge between our goals
and God's will.

Spiritual Serendipity might be thought of as a
spiritually toned self-help book. It is a radical
and contrarian book in that it suggests a nearly
opposite approach to the traditional self-help
panaceas of "positive mental attitude" and
"time management."

For many, positive attitude is essentially a
self-con. We tell ourselves we can *control* everything and *do* anything, while in fact most circumstances and most people are beyond our
control; and without a higher insight and guidance, we ourselves are extremely limited in
doing anything of real significance. Serendip-

ity wants us to see the opportunity and the beauty in things as they really are instead of naively wishing things were different, and to seek and trust God's power rather than our own.

The problem with time management is that time is like tides or currents. It needs to be used and harnessed, not *managed*. It is far better to learn attitudes that help us use time and flow with it than techniques for trying to manage it. (Great rowing techniques don't help when rowing upstream in rapids.) There is a natural (and supernatural) ebb and flow to time. Time has eddies and slow, stretched moments when certain things can happen— things that could not be forced at other times. Serendipity teaches us to respect time rather than manipulate it—to shift directions within its flow and to use its power rather than thrash against it.

On one level, serendipity is the ability to notice what others miss—to observe and appreciate beauty, to sense needs and opportunities, to be receptive to impressions, intuitions, and insights. On a higher level, serendipity of the spirit is receptiveness to inputs beyond our senses—to the deeper nudges and inspirations that come to our hearts and our souls.

Part 1

The Plight, the Problem, and the Promise

Serendip

At the end of the twentieth century

The Plight
(of Those Who Live in Our World)

On this emerald-green, high-mountained
island
in the indigo-blue Indian Ocean
("Sri Lanka" *means* resplendent isle)
workers are fortunate if they earn
100 rupees per week (just under $4).
With that (and the fish they catch
or the rice they grow)
they feed large families.
Yet, as in many poor parts of the world,
people's faces reflect more joy
than discouragement.
Nowhere have I seen a higher ratio
of smiling, open countenances,
childlike in the positive sense that they
never look away from your glance.
Their own glances
are layered with light.
Faces that look out at you
with no self-consciousness
and invite you to look right back in.
The concerns here are as simple as they are
severe:
food to eat, a roof,
and shelter in the monsoon season,

basic health care,
and education for the children.

Sri Lankans are an intelligent, joyful people.
Most returning tourists come back as much
for the people
as for the perfect beaches
and cool, jungle mountains.

Because the pace is slow, and the contrasts
vivid,
(and because my word was born here)
this is a good place to think
about the Three Princes and Horace Walpole.
And it is a clear-perspective place
from which to look back and think about
our world,
yours and mine,
the world of Western civilization as it enters
the twenty-first century. . . .

Our world
is boisterously busy!
(and confusingly complex).
Options, opportunities, and obligations
proliferate and
grow like grass
and most problems stem from surplus
rather than scarcity.

Our windows
(they're still rectangular and made of glass but
now
we turn them on and off with a switch
and change their view with a wireless remote)
show us our competitors and
make us materialistic,
conjuring new wants and then disguising them
as needs.

We find that
trying to do it all and have it all and be it all
won't work.
Because there's no time.
No time for "choose to do's"
because the "have to do's"
and the red-tape and responsibilities
swallow up the tiny time allotment of the
every day.

We try to prepare, to prioritize, and to plan.
We make our lists and try to control the
events
that swirl around us,
but nothing ever goes quite as we planned.
Impediments and interruptions
knock us off course
and turn our planners into
testaments of our failures.

Work and family and personal needs
jerk at each other
like a three-way tug of war.
We look around us
and try for comfort (or at least company)
in the fact
that everyone has the same stress, the same
frustration,
the same unbalance.

Part of the problem is that,
woven in and wound around
the accepted thinking
in our society,
is the dangerously stiff and brittle thread
of *quantity*.
We measure (and are measured)
more by how much we do
than by how well we do it;
more by explicit external exhibit
than by invisible internal insight;
more on our breadth than by our depth;
more on our doing and our getting than on
our being;
more on more . . .
more on quantity than on quality.

Success is outer accumulation and position
rather than inner character,
ownership rather than stewardship,
recognition rather than relationships.

And we sometimes reserve our respect
for those who *win*, who acquire, who run
things,
forgetting or undervaluing less visible gifts
like sensitivity, spontaneity, and even charity.

So how do we change this system,
this society?
We don't.
What we change is our susceptibility to it,
our stereotyped subscription to its standard,
our dependence on its approval.
What we change is
ourselves.

And the tool
that turns and times the transition
is something this book calls
spiritual serendipity.

The Problem
*(of Our Time, Our Place,
and Our Culture)*

We are a people free and mightily blessed
with almost limitless variety and diversity.
Compared with our forefathers,

we can choose among so many different
lifestyles,
so many different causes, careers,
concentrations,
and circumstances.

With all these blessings, how can we be
frustrated or confused?
Surprise: It is *because* of all we have
that many are perplexed.
More expectations demand more
performance.
More desires demand more work.
More education demands more money.
More needs seem to demand more time.
e. e. cummings may have said it best:
"more, more, more, more, more
My hell, what are we anyway—morticians?"
More expectations, desires, and needs
lead us inevitably to the perplexing questions
of *How* and *Why*.
How do we find the time?
Why can't we ever feel satisfied?
How can we have "outer success" (job, career)
and "inner success" (family, character)?
Why, with technology and
"labor-saving devices,"
are we busier than ever?
How do we handle life's unpredictability?
Why is it so difficult to set
clear long-range goals?

How can we be disciplined and structured
and yet retain some spontaneity and flexibility?
Why does time seem to pass ever faster?
How do we handle life's surprises?
Why do relationships die
before we know they are wounded?
How do we raise moral children
in an amoral world?
Why do opportunities pass by
before we can see them clearly?
How do we discover our unique niche,
our individual destiny?
Why, when we have more of everything,
do we seem to have less of joy?
How do we conform our lives to God's will?
Why do we spend so much more effort on
things
than on people?
How can we know if we've made the right
choices
and are "climbing the right mountain"?
Why do we live, *why* do we love,
why are we here?

What kind of questions are these?
They are the *root* questions
of life!
On their answers hang our happiness here
and our station in the hereafter.
But too many questions—can the whole list
be compacted into one?

Sometimes the spiritual context both
supersedes
and simplifies . . .
equaling a single question:
*How can we request and receive
the guidance of God?*

If we view an unlimited, personal Heavenly
Father,
loving us, caring,
wanting to guide us, prompt us,
enlighten us . . .
but committed to our agency,
thus not interfering, not taking the initiative
from us . . .
If we view our very limited selves,
operating under a veil, aware of only
a thin slice
of reality, a tiny percentage of variables,
knowing too little to sort out our own destiny
and make key decisions
without divine guidance . . .
If we view things this way,
then life is not so much about our own skills
or our ability
to schedule and scheme and sort out success.
Instead, it is about our *receptivity*
and our own ability to request and quest for
light.
And both growth and joy are

more about being perceptive
than competitive,
more about being guided
than about being gifted.
And we should worry more
about not feeling than about not failing.

The challenge of a more spiritual paradigm is
to rise above
the usual treadmill
of comparing and competing,
the usual pattern
of praying deeply only in crisis,
the usual life of essentially drifting into things,
of letting circumstances or envy
or paths of least resistance
decide our direction
instead of shafts of light from above.
(Or at least insightful glimpses from within.)

The Promise
(of a More Peaceful,
More Productive Paradigm)

There is an attitude that can change
the way we see life
and the way we *live* life.
It is an attitude that involves new awareness,

new approaches,
and a fresh answer
to the deepest and oldest questions
of how personal guidance is obtained.

We ask: How do we avail ourselves of the
insight, impressions, intuitions, inspirations
that belief in God tells us
must be possible?
"Ask for it" goes the short answer.
But to be effectual,
asking must be accompanied by an
awareness . . .
by an approach or an *attitude*
that helps us ask the right questions and then
hear (and see and feel)
the unexpected answers.
The attitude can be easily named,
but will take
this whole book
to explain.
It is *spiritual serendipity*.

Spiritual serendipity is not a program
or a technique or a method
or "six steps" or a "sequence of actions."
It's not about how to do something,
or even about what to do.
In fact,
it doesn't have to do with doing.

It has to do with
being.
The changes it advocates are not *out*,
in our actions,
but *in*, in our spirits.
A new attitude, deeply understood,
does more than change *what we do*.
It becomes a part of us and thus
it changes *who we are*.

Serendipity of the spirit requires shifts
in our paradigm.
It suggests a new way of looking at ourselves,
our world,
and our relationship with the Being
who made both.

The attitude holds forth promises so grand
that their mere mention breeds skepticism.
But they are listed anyway
in the hope that your "keep reading" interest
will grow faster
than your "stop reading" skepticism.
Spiritual serendipity,
besides opening you to greater guidance
and incremental inspiration, can:

☐ Relax you, reduce your frustration and
stress,
☐ Increase life's excitement, remove boredom,

☐ Sensitize you to beauty
and deepen your feelings,
☐ Orient you to ideas
and increase your creativity,
☐ Make you more *people*-oriented
(and less *things*-oriented),
☐ Strengthen your beliefs in the Divine,
☐ Let you see more
of life's amusement and ironies,
☐ Make you more flexible, more spontaneous,
more *fun*,
☐ Make your life longer
(time seems to slow down
for those who are highly observant and
aware . . .
and a calm spirit contributes to longevity),
☐ Give you peace and joy,
☐ Make you a better parent, a better spouse,
a better friend.

Forgive the expression of what spiritual
serendipity *does*
before the explanation of what it *is* . . .
but the latter will take a while.

Best to begin with "mental serendipity,"
which comes of sharpened senses
and agile awareness
and is accessible
to anyone who takes the time
to understand and apply.

Then can be approached
the extended concept
of spiritual serendipity
which can unlock the stronger doors
and which is accessible only to those who seek
the higher power
and gain the gift.
But first,
let's discover the word itself. To do so
we need to go back to the word's birth,
back more than two hundred years to England
and to
Horace Walpole.

Part 2

Walpole: His Nature, His World, and His Word

London

Midway through the eighteenth century

Horace Walpole, in a letter written in 1754 to
Horace Mann (it must have been a popular first
name), commented on his attraction to "The
Three Princes of Serendip," whom he had read
about in an ancient Persian fable:

*They were always making discoveries, by accidents
and by sagacity, of things of value that they were not
in quest of.* *

What kind of a man was this Walpole? Did
his interest in the concept of serendipity and
his intrigue with a fanciful fable spring from
the type of person he was?

Walpole was born in 1717, the son of Sir
Robert Walpole who would later become England's prime minister. He grew up a son of
privilege and leisure, a product of Eton and
Kings College, Cambridge. Leaving the uni-
versity, he set out on a two-and-a-half-year
tour of France. While he was abroad, his father
had him elected to Parliament. His life was
the epitome of the privileges of noble birth
in eighteenth-century England. But Walpole
seemed to derive productivity and widespread
interests from his ease rather than compla-
cency and laziness. Antiquary, novelist, poli-
tician, poet-master, social charmer, architect,

Brewer's Dictionary of Phrase and Fable, Centenary Edition, 1977.

gardener, and political chronicler all became his appropriate descriptions. Always appreciative of the unique and unpredictable, he designed and built a Gothic castle in which he lived and wrote. His environment inspired mysterious stories of romance and intrigue that made him into what some call "the father of the gothic novel" and influenced the writing of Scott, Byron, Keats, and Coleridge. His insightful and voluminous letters and correspondence give us the clearest picture we have of the social and political life of eighteenth-century England.

Hugh Honour, in his book on *Writers and Their Work*, called Walpole "one of the most delightful characters who ever put pen to paper. He knew everyone worth knowing in his elegant age. He had a substantial passion for antiquities, architecture, printing, letter-writing—everything that could enhance the pleasure of life."

You and I may not have much in common with this man who was born into wealth and position, but he had a freshness that we can all admire, and knowing a little about his nature is helpful in understanding the word he coined.

Some of Walpole's literary peers and contemporaries lend personal insight: Macaulay said that "Walpole rejected, with gay abandon, whatever appeared dull, while retaining only what was in itself amusing or could be made so

by the artifice of his diction." James Boswell
spoke of "Harry's constitutional tranquility or
affection of it." Gilly Williams, who knew him
from boyhood said, "I can figure no being happier than Harry." Thackeray who, like many,
felt that Walpole's correspondence was his
greatest legacy and contribution, said, "Nothing can be more charming than Horace's letters. Fiddles sing all through them: wax lights,
fine dresses, fine jokes, fine plates glitter and
sparkle. There never was such a brilliant, jig-
gling, smirking Vanity Fair as that through
which he leads us.*

What was it about Walpole that gave him his
tranquility, or his happiness, or his gift for seeing life as a graphic, sparkling, exciting adventure? Was it an attitude—an attitude he already
had and for which he found a *name* when he
read the fable of the three princes?

As interesting as the views of friends and literary peers might be, Walpole's own words and
self-description carry even more insight. In a
letter to H. S. Conway, dated June 28, 1760, he
writes:

*I have papers to sort; I have letters and books to
write; I have my prints to paste, my house to build,*

*Hugh Honour, *Writers and Their Work*, F. Mildner &
Sons, London, 1957.

*and everything in the world to tell posterity—how
am I to find time for all this?*

And a few more examples, again from Honour:

*I love to communicate my satisfactions. My melan-
choly I generally shut up in my own breast.*

*This world is comedy to those that think, a tragedy
to those that feel.*

*In short, the true definition of me is that I am a
dancing senator—not that I do dance, or do anything by being a senator; but I go to balls and to the
House of Commons—to look on, and you will believe me when I tell you that I really think the former is the more serious occupation of the two: at
least the performers are more in earnest.*

*What should we gain by triumph [over the
colonists]? Would America laid waste, deluged with
blood, plundered and enslaved, replace America
flourishing, rich, and free?*

This man, then, who seemed interested in
everything, who loved fun and spontaneity,
who was open and candid about his own feelings and weaknesses, who was part cynic, part
political critic, part romanticist, and who was
always trying to discover what was inside himself as well as the world around him—this man

coined the word "serendipity." The concept of happy accidents and good things discovered through awareness and sagacity appealed to him because so much interested him and because life held such adventure and intrigue for him.

Perhaps the most revealing of all Walpole's insights was the occasion when he tried to see himself through the eyes of one Reverend Mr. Steward, a fellow guest at the country home of the Earl of Hartford.

Strolling about the house, he saw me first sitting on the pavement of the lumber room with Louis, all over cobwebs and dirt and mortar; then found me in his own room on a ladder writing on a picture; and half an hour afterwards lying on the grass in the court with the dogs and the children, in my slippers and without my hat. He had some doubt whether I was the painter or the workman from the factory or the tutor for the family's children; but you would have died at his surprise when he saw me walk into dinner in formal dress and sit by Lady Hartford.

Lord Lyttelton was there and the conversation turned to literature. Finding me not quite ignorant added to the Reverend's wonder; but when he saw me go to romps and jumping with the two boys, he could stand it no longer and begged to know who and what sort of man I really was, for he had never met with anything of the kind.*

*Honour, op. cit.

It appears that Walpole *cultivated* an attitude of awareness, unpredictability, spontaneity, and joy, and that he relished the unexpected, the happy discoveries and surprises of life. Perhaps he found slight frustration in the fact that there was no word to describe the attitude or quality that he most valued.

Then he came upon an ancient Persian fable called "The Three Princes of Serendip." In the story he found a clear expression of his attitude and in the title he found the root for a new word.

Part 3

The Three Princes of Serendip

Persia

Early in the fifth century

Prologue

I have been searching off and on for a copy of this fable for twenty years, and I now hold it in my hands. The story itself is a fairy tale, set in the fifth century A.D. in the royal days of Anuradhapura on the island of Ceylon, which we now call Sri Lanka but which was then called Serendip. It was the time of the Sassanian empire in Persia and of the famous dynasties of Gupta and Vakatakas in India. The original fable was passed from one generation to the next and acquired several different versions. All were essentially about the gift of finding valuable or agreeable things not sought after.

I am at the British Library in the British Museum in the heart of London. There are eleven million volumes here, some of which line the wall, three stories high, that encircles the round reading room where I sit under the huge gold and blue dome that arches eighty feet above my head. William Wordsworth sat here to write. So did Karl Marx.

This copy was printed in Russell Street, Covent Garden, London. It is an old volume, published in England in 1722 for a man named Will Chetwood. It is as old as the copy that Walpole read. It could conceivably *be* the copy that he read. The cover is old leather, polished by the hands that have held it over the years. It was translated from a French edition that had been published earlier in Amsterdam. The French had been translated from the original Persian.

What follows is my own minimally retranslated version. Read it to yourself; try to read it with the same interest and insight with which Walpole read it, and, if you get a chance, read it to a child.

The Three Princes
of Serendip:
a fable

*T*here is a land far off, at the
very end of the earth, called Serendip—a resplendent island where
tall trees grew on emerald mountains. Long,
long ago on Serendip, there lived a great and
wise king called Jafer.

King Jafer had three sons. When each was
born, a strange and beautiful bird with golden
wings and eyes like fire dipped low out of the
sky, but was seen only by a handful of children
near the ancient Mountain of Great Serenity.

The king wanted to prepare his sons well so
that they could someday become good rulers
of Serendip. He wanted them to learn three
things: virtue, science, and wisdom. Being a
wise man himself, he asked even wiser men and
women, both of his own country and of other
lands, to come and teach his sons.

But few teachers would come from other
countries because the ocean that surrounded
Serendip was filled with great and fearsome
dragons—sea monsters who attacked ships
with their sharp claws and slapped holes in the

hulls with their long, whipping tales. The teachers who did come from other lands were therefore filled with courage as well as knowledge, and they taught the boys to see and perceive with both their eyes and their hearts.

The three princes were good students. Their teachers taught them much virtue, science, and wisdom . . . as well as grammar, languages, poetry, and music. They also taught the management and handling of elephants, the most important and useful animal in Serendip.

When the three princes were no longer boys but young men, King Jafer decided to interview them (and to test them) one at a time. To the eldest prince he said, "I want you now to be king," holding his own crown over the boy's head. The prince noticed that his father's fingers held the crown very tightly, and he said, "With respect, Father, I decline. I am not yet prepared to rule."

When the middle prince came in, the king got up off his throne and offered the magnificent chair to the son, saying that it was time for a new king. The prince listened carefully and heard how strong and clear the king's voice was and told him that he was still a great and able king and could rule yet for many years.

Then the king sent for the youngest prince and asked him to be king. The young prince observed the sparkle in the king's eyes and knew it was a test. "Oh, no, Great King. I am yet a boy and your eyes are still clear, and your mind strong."

King Jafer was pleased—each of his sons had wisdom and modesty. He decided to complete their education by sending them abroad, for he knew that until they had seen other parts of the earth they would not realize how many good people there are in the world, or how many good ideas, or how many different ways there are of thinking, of living, and of being. He hoped that, in addition to enhanced perspective, they might complete a quest that would free his kingdom of the curse of its dragon-infested waters.

He called them to him and said: "My beloved sons, the ancients have said that the mists of yesteryear were marvelously distilled into a magic formula, written in one hundred lines of verse upon a single scroll. The formula-poem is called *Death to Dragons*. A liquid potion can be made by following it, which, when poured into the oceans, will poison and kill the dragons that surround our island. I send you forth to find *Death to Dragons*. Do not return until you find it or until you have my permission to come home."

The three princes, wearing plain clothing and riding unadorned elephants (for they felt they would learn more if they could not be recognized as princes) set off on their journey. As they started their trek to the sea, they *noticed*, more than ever before, the *beauty* of Serendip. They knew they would miss their home and their father, but they were determined to find *Death to Dragons*.

The journey across the ocean to India was a dangerous one, but the princes found a large and fast boat and made it safely across. During the journey they saw several of the ugly and ferocious sea dragons riding upon the waves.

On the other side, the princes began to ask questions and to search for anyone who knew of the formula in *Death to Dragons*. They were adept at asking questions and they did so in such a polite and fair-spoken way that people were naturally inclined to like them and to try to help them. They were directed to a grizzled old sage who had heard of a mysterious one-hundred-line poem. "There is only one copy in all the world," he told them. "It is in the keeping of an ancient seer with strange, shining eyes. His name is Aphoenicius and he carries the poem in a silver cylinder and guards it always. He has a hundred disguises and is at times invisible. He never stays in one place for more than one night."

"Have you ever seen Aphoenicius?" asked the eldest prince.

"He stayed with me one night," said the sage, "and because you are so courteous and because I believe you seek the poem for a noble purpose, I will tell you what I know. At night Aphoenicius spoke in his sleep and said what I believe to be two lines from the magic verse:

Though the treasure saline be,
You will not scoop it from the sea.

The princes wrote down the lines, thanked the sage, and continued their journey.

ventually they entered the land of Persia, which was ruled by the powerful King Behram, and purchased camels to cross the desert. In midjourney they passed a caravan and were asked by the caravan master if they had seen a camel that had been lost. The eldest prince said, "No, we have seen no camel except those we ride. But may I ask you, Did your camel have only one eye?"

"Yes," said the master. "Then you have seen him."

"No," said the eldest, "we saw no camel. But did the one you lost have a tooth missing from the front of his mouth?"

"Yes," said the master. "You are joking with me. Show me where my camel is."

"We've not seen it," insisted the first prince. "But did it have a lame hind leg?"

With that, the caravan master, convinced that these young men had stolen his camel, had them arrested and brought to court.

King Behram, hearing of the case and finding it interesting, decided to sit in judgment personally. The three princes were not allowed to speak, but there were many witnesses who had heard the eldest prince describe the camel completely, and thus it appeared that they must be guilty. Regretfully (because the young men were polite and upright) the king sentenced them to die, as the law demanded. But Behram was a good king, inclined toward leniency, and offered to pardon them if they would return the camel. The princes could only repeat that they had never seen the camel.

Just then a great bird with golden wings and shining eyes swooped low in the sky. Only one old woman saw it, but immediately afterward the lost camel's owner burst into the courtroom saying that his neighbor had found the camel and begged forgiveness for his false accusation of the three princes.

King Behram, embarrassed by his improper judgment and impressed with the three brothers (who had never revealed their identity as princes) invited them to his castle and asked them to explain how they knew so much about a camel they had never seen.

The eldest prince graciously did so:

"Where we saw tracks, we observed that the grass was nibbled on only one side of the road, so we knew the camel had lost an eye. Along the road we noticed partly chewed bits of grass and concluded that the camel was dropping them through the gap of a missing tooth. And in the tracks themselves, we saw evidence of a dragging rear leg. We know even more than we told, Great King. We know that the camel carried butter and honey. We noticed ants, which seek after fat on the left of the road, and flies, which seek after sweet on the right."

Delighted and even more impressed, King Behram invited them to stay at his palace for a time. They agreed to do so, and continued to ask everyone they met about the old man with shining eyes who carried the formula in *Death to Dragons*. Because they were so friendly, and because their motive in wanting the formula was unselfish and altruistic (to save their island from fierce sea dragons), everyone wanted to help them, but few had heard of old Aphoenicius and his silver cylinder.

One evening, at a dinner attended by
several of King Behram's ministers
and viziers, the three princes were
sitting together and, as they often did, discussing their feelings and the impressions that
sometimes came mysteriously to their minds.
The eldest said that he sensed that the wine
they were drinking came from a vineyard that
grew on a sepulcher or cemetery. The youngest
prince said he felt that the mutton they were
eating came from a lamb that had been raised
and suckled by a dog rather than a ewe sheep.
The middle brother said that he wished his
own impression was as harmless as these, but
alas, it was not. He perceived that one particular vizier, seated there in the dining room, had
malicious and seditious thoughts and was perhaps plotting to take the life of King Behram.

The king, sitting across the table, heard his
name mentioned and insisted that the three
princes tell him their entire conversation.
When they had done so, King Behram asked
them how they were able to perceive such
things, and they told him that it was by what
they observed and by what they felt in their
hearts and minds. The first prince, for example, told him that he had experienced a peculiar
and sad feeling as he tasted the wine and then
had glimpsed a vineyard-cemetery in his mind.
The third prince explained that the mutton

tasted slightly unusual and put him somehow in mind of a dog. The second brother said he had noticed one of the viziers change color as the king had spoken earlier of punishing the guilty, and that the vizier's eyes, full of maliciousness and indignation, had not left the king since.

The next day, King Behram checked the accuracy of the princes' feelings. He summoned the wine master, who confirmed that the wine had come from a vineyard planted over a sepulcher. He summoned the shepherd, who told him a story of how a wolf had killed a ewe sheep leaving a tiny lamb, which had been suckled and raised by the shepherd's dog. And in checking court records, he found that the angry vizier had a son who had been banished from the country as punishment for a crime.

Amazed and impressed, the king went to the three princes to ask their advice on how to discover or escape from the vizier's plot of revenge. The second son said he had observed that the vizier had a lady friend to whom he probably revealed his plans.

King Behram located the lady, befriended her, and flattered her with promises of position and gifts. She told him of the vizier's plot, which involved presenting a jeweled cup to the king at the next state dinner and then proposing a toast to his health. The jeweled cup was to contain poison.

When the night of the dinner came and the vizier presented the jeweled cup, the king said, "So much feeling comes with the cup that I cannot accept it until you drink from it first." In horror the vizier confessed by saying, "I am fallen into a misfortune that I had prepared for others." King Behram, urged by his ministers to put the traitor to death, insisted on consulting first with the three princes. They advised him to show compassion and to imagine how he would feel if he had a son and if his son, like the vizier's, had been banished. Thus the king adopted an attitude of empathy and arranged for the vizier to be banished rather than executed—banished to the same land where his son had previously been sent.

Before his banishment, the repentant vizier went to the three princes to voice his gratitude. In their conversation, the princes asked if he had any knowledge of the ancient sage with shining eyes who carried the secret of *Death to Dragons*. The vizier recalled once spending a night in an inn with such a man, who in his sleep had muttered a portion of a verse so curious that the Vizier had committed it to memory:

And often from the sight is hidden
Such magic not by self-love bidden.

For saving his life, King Behram offered the princes any three wishes that he could grant.

They replied that their only wish was to serve him well and to be his friends.

*S*hortly thereafter, King Behram called the three brothers to his side to ask them a great favor. "When my grandfather was king," he explained, "he possessed the great Mirror of Justice, which had the power to reflect both truth and falsehood. Whenever there was a dispute in the land, the two arguing or opposing parties were made to look into the mirror. The rightful or truthful party was reflected as he was, but the wrong or dishonest person was reflected in the mirror with a face of dark purple. The guilty party could return to his former complexion only if he went down into a deep pit for forty days with only bread and water and then came forth and confessed his error to everyone. Because of the mirror there was justice in the land. People dealt with each other fairly and thus grew prosperous and happy."

The three princes listened attentively and with great fascination. (Indeed, listening was among their greatest skills.) The king explained that his father and uncle had fought over the throne after his grandfather's death. When his father won the battle and became king, the uncle, in bitterness, had stolen the Mirror of

Justice, taken it to the far coast of India and sold it to a young king.

The mirror ceased to reflect justice when it was taken out of Persia, but the Indian king who purchased it found that it did something else, also of great value. In his kingdom, a large and terrible five-fingered *hand* rose from the ocean's horizon each morning and hung ominously in the sky beneath the sun all day. In the evening it suddenly descended, grabbed a man from the city or the shore, and hurled him into the sea. The Indian king discovered that, when the mirror was held up to reflect the hand, it changed its behavior, grabbing instead a pig or a dog or some other animal each day to cast into the sea.

King Behram explained that a young queen now ruled the Indian kingdom—a daughter of the king who had bought the mirror. King Behram said that he had petitioned her to return the mirror, but she had steadfastly refused except on condition that someone succeed in destroying or disposing of the hand. "Now," said King Behram, "with my great confidence in you three brothers, I am asking you to go and conquer the hand and then bring the Mirror of Justice back to me."

Without any plan or foreknowledge of what they would do, but with faith in their own ingenuity and in the power and intuition that seemed to guide them, the three princes ac-

cepted the challenge of the king. They also
hoped that at the far coast of India they could
find further clues in their quest for *Death to
Dragons.* After brief preparations, they took
their leave.

After seeing them off, King Behram walked
back to his palace, noticing with great joy the
beauty of the fields and forests around him and
the rich color and textures of the baskets and
rugs made by the people in the villages he
passed. He stopped along the way to pray for
the welfare and success of his three young
friends and thus found himself following their
example and their advice to be *watchful, appreciative, and prayerful.*

A few days after the princes had
left, a merchant, knowing of the
king's great love for music, came
to the palace and exhibited before King Behram some instruments and musical treasures
brought from faroff lands. In the merchant's
company was a young woman of such appeal-
ing grace and beauty that the king could not
take his eyes from her. Inquiring, he was told
that she was Diliramma, a young woman of unknown origin whom the traders had found as a
small girl, abandoned in the forest, dressed in
blue silk, and wearing a curious necklace of

tiny interlocking silver crowns. The merchant had adopted her as a foster daughter. The king, overwhelmed by her beauty, said to the merchant, "She is not of the number who has need of ornaments to set herself off. Rather, the ornaments have need of her to make them more bright and glittering."

Only then was the king informed that Diliramma was also a singer. She was summoned and sang before the king in a way that filled him with such rapture that he could only say, "You have equally charmed my eyes and my ears."

Unsurprisingly, the king offered to make her the palace musician and give her sumptuous apartments in the palace. The merchant, pleased at his foster daughter's good fortune, quickly agreed.

In the days that followed, King Behram was in bliss, hunting in the royal woods by day and listening each evening to Diliramma's songs. He reflected that the only thing that could add to his happiness would be for the three princes to return with the magic mirror.

One morning he invited Diliramma to go on a hunt with him. She agreed, and off they went with a hundred servants, riding the great royal elephants. Most of those who surrounded the king were fearful and subordinate—quick to agree with him and striving to say to him only what he wanted to hear. But Diliramma was

different, joking and laughing and saying exactly what she truly thought and felt.

After observing the hunt for a time, and seeing what an exceptional archer the king was,
she gave him a challenge. "I would like," she
said, "to see you pierce both the hoof and the
ear of a deer with a single arrow."

Great marksman though he was, the king
thought the task was impossible . . . until he
remembered the attitude of the three princes
who always looked for a creative or innovative
way to do everything. He thought for a moment, then shot an arrow that grazed and tick-
led the deer's ear. The deer lifted his hind leg
to scratch his ear and as it did, the king let fly
another arrow which pierced the deer's ear and
its hoof. The courtiers and servants cheered
and clapped, not only for the king's skill but for
his stratagem. Diliramma was also impressed,
but she winked and said, "You have deceived
both the deer and me and succeeded only
through a trick." In sudden silence, all eyes
were turned to Diliramma and to the king,
whose face turned red with embarrassment and
temper. He was not used to any form of criti-
cism or to anyone joking with him. On impulse
and in anger he stripped off her cloak and rode
off yelling back at his guards to leave her alone
in the deepest part of the forest.

When the king arrived back at the palace, he
realized what he had done, and inside of him a

great conflict arose between anger and love. Love said, "For an indiscretion, for a *trifle*, you treat so cruelly the most beautiful person in the world? Bring her back!" Anger replied, "No, you cannot resent this indignity too much! If you recall her will you not be thought like the weathercock that turns with every wind?"

Recognizing the truth of the first voice, King Behram sent all of his guards to find and bring back Diliramma. But they returned at nightfall, reporting that she was nowhere to be found. Imagining that she had been eaten by a wild beast, the king was heartbroken and felt the terrible burden of guilt. He became very ill, and as days passed his condition grew steadily worse.

*I*n the meantime, the three princes were experiencing a very challenging journey to the far coasts of India in their quest to find and recover the Mirror of Justice. They reached a wide river, which was the boundary of the coastal kingdom. On their side, on the steep rocky hillside that faced the river, was an ancient monastery. The abbot in charge was impressed with the polite behavior of the three princes but became very concerned when they told him of their quest to vanquish the great hand and recover the magic mirror. He told them of a demon who lived underground in the forest on the opposite bank of the river—a demon who took delight in protecting the great hand and who could look up through the earth and see the intent in men's eyes. "I have observed others who came to fight the hand," said the abbot. "If the under-earth demon sees intent to destroy the hand, he pushes the ground up, causing trees to fall and boulders to roll, knocking the men from their horses and either burying them or swallowing them into deep cracks in the earth."

The third prince, always full of courage, said he would cross alone to test the danger. He hired a boat and crossed the river, but just as he stepped to the shore the ground began to heave. Huge stones tumbled in his direction and tall forest trees fell toward him. He scrambled back into the boat and paddled back out into the river just in time.

The other two princes watched from the opposite bank, frightened and confused by what they saw. They pulled their brother to safety and all three returned to the monastery, where they asked the abbot if there was any way to get past the demon.

The abbot told them of the monastery's great library and said he believed that most every answer could be found in books. For the next several days the abbot and the three princes researched and studied. All they could find was one ancient passage that reminded the princes of the verses in *Death to Dragons*. It said:

> *One feather from a peacock's tail*
> *In wisdom's hand may oft prevail.*

Since it was the best they could find, the abbot presented each of the three princes with a beautiful peacock's tail feather and said, "It is possible to follow even a clouded or dark saying part of the way."

Not feeling that they could wait any longer, the princes hired a boat and set out to cross the river, hoping that something in their sagacity or intuition would help them get past the under-earth demon. They made the river crossing in silence, each searching his mind for a strategy. Just as they neared the other bank, the middle prince noticed that his peacock feather had dots on it that looked like blue eyes. "Let me go first," he said. "I have an idea." He climbed from the boat, holding his feather over his eyes like a mask. He could see through the feather's tiny cracks, but the under-earth demon saw only the flat, blue eyes of the peacock feather and could not see the intent in the prince's real eyes. The earth remained still and calm. The other princes followed his example, and all passed through the forest safely.

On the other side they sought out and found

the young queen of the coastal kingdom, who dazzled them with her beauty and courtesy and quickly agreed that they should have the Mirror of Justice if they could conquer the evil hand.

That evening the queen took them to the seacoast where they saw, low in the eastern sky, the terrifying sight of a huge suspended hand. As the sun set, the hand swooped toward the beach. As it did, one of the queen's guards held up the Mirror of Justice. The hand changed direction, grabbed a milk cow from the nearby field, and hurled it far out into the ocean.

The following morning the three brothers went to the seacoast and observed the great five-fingered hand rising in the sky just beneath the sun and gradually moving across the sky.

The day wore on, and still the princes could develop no plan of action. Just as evening fell, a golden winged bird with shining eyes flew silently overhead. Only the youngest prince noticed. Suddenly, without warning, he stepped out onto the beach and asked the guard to lay the mirror aside. As he did, the sun set and the hand suddenly swept down directly toward the youngest prince. As the huge hand came closer with all five of its fingers extended, the young prince held up his own right hand with two fingers extended and the others curled together. Immediately, the hand veered off its course and plunged into the sea, sinking into the depths like a stone. The other two princes rushed to their brother, who explained that a strong impression had come to him that the hand's message was that five men, perfectly united in an evil cause, could destroy the world. His response was that two people, perfectly united in worthy purpose, could overcome all evil and master the universe.

The young queen, who had watched the drama, rushed forward, congratulating the young prince and exclaiming, "Everywhere, true courage meets with quick respect." He repeated to her the message his two fingers had sent to the hand—that two people, perfectly united, could overcome all evil in the universe.

The queen quickly kept her end of the bargain by giving the three princes the Mirror of Justice. She begged them to stay at her palace for a day or two before returning to King Behram and they consented.

That evening they celebrated the demise of the hand at a great palace party. The princes noticed that the queen, despite her joy in her country's deliverance from the hand, still had a look of sadness that occasionally flickered in her dark and lovely eyes. Later, when the other guests had gone home, the princes asked her to share her hidden sorrow.

She told them she had once had an elder sister called Padmini who had been her best

friend. One afternoon long ago, on a day when
they were wearing identical blue silk dresses
and necklaces of tiny interlocking silver crowns,
a fierce nomadic tribe charged them as they
frolicked together and stole Padmini away.
Guards had pursued the kidnappers and finally
caught them three days later. But by then the
evil men, hoping to escape the guards, had left
Padmini in a dense forest. She had never been
found.

Deeply touched, the eldest prince said, "As a
vine bowed with the weight of grapes, we are
honored to share your grief."

The three princes then told the queen of
their quest for *Death to Dragons* and asked if
she had ever seen or heard of the old sage
called Aphoenicius, the keeper of the silver
cylinder.

After a moment's thought, the queen recalled the strange but kind man with shining eyes who had whispered to her a short
verse shortly after her sister Padmini had been
taken.

> *One may seek but cannot borrow*
> *This mystery lying close to sorrow.*

Recognizing the words as another piece in
the puzzle of *Death to Dragons*, the princes
wrote them down with the other clues they
had collected and, leaving the beautiful young

queen their fondest wishes and best regards, departed the next morning to carry the prized Mirror of Justice back to King Behram.

As was their practice, the princes tried to observe everything and to learn all they could during their journey. On their way, they came to a small village and decided to spend the night there. They made friends with several of the villagers and were introduced to the village chief. They noticed the worry and anxiety in his face and asked if there was any help or assistance they could give. The chief told them of a rumor that Drakir, the three-headed serpent, had broken loose from his cage high on top of Prison Mountain. Drakir had been captured and imprisoned many generations before by the people of this very village—by the ancestors of the chief and the other villagers who now told the tale of his escape to the three princes.

"The high Prison Mountain is very far away, and if Drakir truly has escaped, it will take some time for him to come. But we must get word to King Behram, for Drakir will surely go there first to get the Standard of Power." They explained that when the ancients had captured Drakir, their leader had been a blacksmith. His leather apron was thought to possess magic. It was called the Standard of Power and was kept at the king's palace. "If Drakir gets the standard," said the village chief, "he will become even more powerful. He will be unstoppable and will take control of all the land."

The three princes told the chief that they were on the way to the king's palace and would extend the warning and safeguard the standard. "Before we go," said the eldest, "is there any more you can tell us of Drakir?" The chief said that they had been warned of Drakir's escape by a strange, elderly traveler with shining eyes who had stayed only one night and had said that the dragon could be overcome only if his three long necks could be twisted together into a single great cord. This would take away his strength. Once his strength was diminished, the great imperial bird, a bird with feathers the color of sky, grass, and sunset, would carry him back to his mountain prison.

Recognizing that the old traveler must have been Aphoenicius, the three princes asked where he had gone and if he had said anything as he slept. The chief said that no one had been with him during the night or seen him leave, but some children had seen a bird with golden wings and shining eyes fly from the house where the old man had slept.

In gratitude and friendship the princes left their peacock feathers with the chief, instructing him to send one of the feathers by runner to the king's palace if trouble ever came to the village. The princes promised that the moment they received one of the feathers, they would rush to the rescue. After making this promise, they set off at a quick pace to return to King Behram.

When the three princes arrived back at King Behram's palace, they were shocked at how very ill the king had become. He lay on his back, white as ash, and could not even lift his head in greeting. The princes, who had been so anxious to present the king with the recovered Mirror of Justice and to warn him of the dragon Drakir's escape, were suddenly concerned only for the king's life and health.

In a feeble voice King Behram told them of Diliramma, of his deep love for her, and of his terrible and angry mistake in leaving her in the woods to die. His guilt and his grief were too deep, he said, and he felt now that he would die.

Quickly the princes presented him with the great mirror, hoping it would lift the weight and gloom from the king. He was pleased, and a tiny flush of color returned to his cheeks, but still he did not lift his head.

Searching for other ways to brighten the king's spirits, the three princes decided to reveal their true identity, knowing that their father was a friend of King Behram. The king managed a slight smile and said he had known that the princes were of noble birth and had received wise tutoring. "Give my regards to your father," he said, "for unless I can overcome this heavy grief I will soon be gone."

Deeply concerned, the three princes went on a long walk together trying to come up with an idea or create some other plan to restore the king's spirits. The eldest said, "Finding a remedy for an affliction of the heart is not as easy as finding a stray camel or uncovering an ugly plot or facing a fearsome hand."

All night they walked and talked. In the morning they went to the king with an idea: "In the seven most spectacular locations in your kingdom, build seven splendid castles. Into each castle put a beautiful princess—a daughter of a neighboring king. Also bring the seven best storytellers in the land and put one in each castle. Use your great wealth and resources to do all of this quickly. Then for one glorious week go to a separate castle each day, first conversing with and getting to know each princess, then listening to the best story of the storyteller."

The idea amused King Behram and distracted him from his own misery. Though still flat on his back, he called in his ministers and started the projects immediately.

*N*ow able to think of something besides the king, the princes turned their attention to the danger of the three-headed serpent. They had not told the sick king of the danger, but they used the authority he had given them to have the Standard of Power attached to the very top of the high flagpole in the center courtyard of the palace. The pole, made of ebony, was very hard and stout. There at the top of the pole, they reasoned, the Standard of Power would be high out of Drakir's reach and in a place where they could keep an eye on it.

*T*he king's engineers constructed the seven palaces in record time, and the king's ambassadors arranged for the seven most beautiful princesses and the seven most creative storytellers to occupy them. The day was set for the king to start his week of visits.

On the night before the king's journey, the three princes sat together discussing their increasing hopes for the king's recovery and their decreasing hopes that they would ever find *Death to Dragons.* The youngest prince glanced out of the window into the moonlit courtyard and gasped as his eyes fell on a fearsome sight. There was Drakir, smoke coming from his three mouths, all six evil little eyes staring up at the Standard of Power high on the ebony pole. As the princes watched from the window, Drakir first tried to burn the pole with a blast of fire from his three red throats. But the thick, hard ebony pole would not burn and the dragon became impatient. Grasping high up on the pole with one mouth, lower with the second, and biting the bottom of the pole with his third mouth, Drakir used his awesome strength to pull the pole right out of the ground.

At that exact moment the princes noticed a fleeting opportunity to do something they had thought would be impossible. They jumped from the window; the eldest grabbed the great dragon's tail and held fast while the middle and youngest princes each seized one end of the long flagpole and ran around and around in a circle, twisting the three snakelike necks together as the three heads continued to hold fast to the pole in defiant anger.

As the necks twisted into one great cord, the dragon's strength drained away and the princes were able to bind the heads together so that the necks could not come untwisted. When they had done so, just as Aphoenicius had promised, an enormous imperial bird with wings of blue, green, and rose, swept out of the night sky, snatched the weakened dragon in his sharp talons, and flew away with him toward the prison place on the distant high mountain.

The next morning, right on schedule, King Behram was carried (he was still unable to walk) to the first of seven castles, which was nestled in a high mountain meadow. The beauty of the place, and the enchantment of the lovely princess who greeted him, lifted his spirits as the three princes had predicted. And the storyteller's tale, later in the evening, was so exciting and engrossing that the king raised his head from his pillow and began to forget his grief and feel some will to live. By the end of the day the king had regained enough strength to sit up in his bed.

Through the days of the week each castle, each princess, and each storyteller was better than the one before, and by the time he reached the seventh castle, the king was able to stand and walk, and some of the light had returned to his eyes.

*T*he three princes had decided to meet the king at the seventh castle, but as they journeyed toward it, they were overtaken by a messenger bearing a peacock feather. Knowing that this was the distress signal from their friends in the small village, they changed course immediately and made haste toward the village, which was at a distance of a few days' journey.

When they finally arrived, they beheld great disaster. Fire had burned the village to the ground. They found the old chief, who told them that several days earlier the villagers had looked up to see the great imperial bird flying over, carrying Drakir toward Prison Mountain. Drakir's evil eyes had seen the village and even in his weakened condition he was able to belch out enough fire from his nostrils as he passed overhead to touch off fire in the village. Strong winds had fanned the flames and the village had been destroyed.

Seeing the misery and the suffering of their friends and brothers, the three princes wept.

"Was any life lost?" asked the eldest.

"Only two people are missing," said the chief, "and neither was a permanent resident of our village. One was the old man with shining eyes who had come again to stay for a single night. The other was a young woman with a beautiful voice whom some villagers had found wandering lost and dazed in the forest some weeks ago. The girl would answer no questions about her identity, but the village nursed her back to health and she had favored them with her lovely singing."

Distraught in realizing that the two who were lost were the very two people they most wanted to find, the princes, after doing all they could for the village, sorrowfully prepared to depart, intent on returning to check on King Behram.

As they left the village, the princes paused to look again at the desolation. As they thought about the villagers who had lost their homes they wept once again, their tears collecting in a hollow on the large boulder where they stood.

When they began looking up, ready to begin their journey, their eyes fell upon a shocking sight. There, in a fire-blackened field near a river stream, was the charred body of a man, burned beyond recognition except for his right forearm and hand, untouched by fire and tightly clutching a silver cylinder.

"The keeper of the secret formula has been killed," they exclaimed, "and though his death brings deep sadness, the magic formula will now be ours."

The eldest pulled the cylinder from the ancient one's fingers and walked down by the stream with his brothers to open it. But what fell from the cylinder was mostly ashes. Only small fragments of the scroll were unburned. The only readable lines were:

> *Though the treasure saline be,*
> *You will not scoop it from the sea.*

> *And often from the sight is hidden*
> *Such magic not by self-love bidden.*

> > *One feather from a peacock's tail*
> > *In wisdom's hand may oft prevail.*

> > *One may seek but cannot borrow*
> > *This mystery lying close to sorrow.*

"After so great a search, we have found only the lines we already know," exclaimed the middle prince. "It was a hundred lines and it is lost forever," said the eldest, casting the cylinder aside.

At that moment they heard a sound up on the bank near where Aphoenicius's burned body lay. Looking up, they saw the ashes stir, and a bird with golden wings and shining eyes rose from the spot. As they watched, the bird swooped down next to them and snatched the silver cylinder from the ground at their feet and carried it in flight to the great boulder where the princes had rested and wept. To their amazement, the bird began scooping up their tears into the silver cylinder. Then it flew off into the east like an eagle.

The princes, perplexed by the bird and saddened that their own quest had failed, continued their journey. After several miles they heard screams coming from a wooded valley beneath the trail. Rushing down they caught a glimpse of a girl racing through the trees, chased by a bear. Their own shouts succeeded in scaring the bear off and they rushed to the frightened girl. Thanking them, she explained that she was a homeless girl who had been kindly cared for by the villagers. After their great loss of homes and food in the fire, however, she felt she would be too much of a burden, so she had left, sneaking away unseen.

The princes asked her if her name was Diliramma and as her eyes widened with apprehension, they assured her that King Behram loved her and had almost died from the grief and guilt of his anger, which he thought had cost her her life.

Overcome with joy she told the princes that she was called Diliramma but that she thought she had had another name . . . so long ago that she could no longer remember it. In gratitude for saving her life, she gave them a gift from around her neck, a small and intricate

necklace made from tiny interlocking silver
crowns.

With great excitement the princes told her
that they now knew her true name: Padmini.
As they explained, Padmini could hardly believe her good fortune: she had now discovered
her own true name and the whereabouts of her
sister, and King Behram loved her and wanted
her back.

he journey back to the king was
pure joy for Padmini. But the
princes had mixed feelings. They
were happy to have helped so many, yet sad
about the failure of their own quest.

As they approached his palace, King Behram
came forward to greet them. The joy he felt
when he saw Diliramma (Padmini) with them
was so intense that even the birds were silent.

In his joy, King Behram found great compassion. He sent the engineers who built his seven
castles to assist in rebuilding the burned village, and he had the food and provisions from
the castles removed and taken to the village.
He sent word to the young queen of the coastal
kingdom that her sister had been found and
was to become his wife . . . and invited her and
all her entourage to come for the wedding
and for a long visit.

To make happy endings even happier, the seven princesses in the seven castles married the seven storytellers, who thus became noblemen and kings.

The three princes were filled with joy for so many, but because their own quest had failed, their hearts felt like plump walnuts bored by hungry worms. But the next day, their spirits were lifted by the arrival of a messenger from their own kingdom informing them that their father now wished them to return.

Joyfully and obediently they said their goodbyes and set out on their journey. King Behram wrote a letter for them to carry to their father. The letter said that the princes brought to his kingdom and to his life "a state of splendor and perfect tranquility."

*T*he princes made great haste until they got to the ocean. They found it so infested with sea dragons that there were no more boatmen and no more boats for hire. Finally they found an abandoned boat and set out on their own. Quickly they were surrounded by sea dragons on all sides and thought their lives would end.

Just then they heard the flutter of great wings. They looked up and saw the golden bird with shining eyes, clutching the silver cylinder in his talons. Down he swooped, letting a spray of liquid spill from the cylinder and into the boiling sea. As the droplets fell on and around the sea dragons they went limp and lifeless and slipped silently down into the depths of the sea.

The princes sailed swiftly across the ocean channel and on the shore of their homeland found elephants to complete the journey to their father's palace. Just as they arrived and embraced their father, messengers also arrived with the news that dead dragons now lined the coast and that no live ones were to be found anywhere in the channel.

After all the dragons were dead, the golden bird sprinkled the rest of the silver cylinder's contents out across the emerald mountains of Serendip. As they fell, the tiny droplets turned into the sapphires, rubies, and opals that still exist in abundance in that land.

As his sons told him of their adventures and travels, the wise old father, King Jafer, laughed with delight as they realized that the princes' tears of compassion for the poor and afflicted were the very potion that brings death to dragons—and the formula described in Aphoenicius's verse.

The princes became wise rulers of Serendip. They governed with their sagacity, with their compassion, and with the insight and inspiration they had learned both to seek and to follow.

Wherever there are people and usually when least expected, the bird with golden wings and shining eyes occasionally dips into sight, but it is seen only by those who are looking up.

Epilogue

As with all good fables, each person who reads
the tale finds his own set of meanings and messages. And when he reads it again, he may find
more.

Walpole felt that serendipity was a quality
that grew within people who, like the three
princes, had a cause or mission and pursued it
with sagacity, sensitivity, and wisdom. But there
are additional lessons—all related to this central theme and to each other. There is the underlying message about the ultimate power of
charity and compassion. There are lessons
about noticing and listening, about feeling
deeply, about wishing only to serve, about how
thinking can be more powerful than *doing*,
about faith and intuition in situations where no
preplan can exist, about being watchful and
prayerful, about thinking creatively and later-
ally, about following hunches and intuition,
about a being of wisdom and inspiration, sometimes in human form, who is only seen by
those who are "looking up," about the answers
and wisdom of books, about the importance of
justice but also about its incompleteness without mercy, about the power of unity and the
value of stories and storytellers, and about how

all we ever really know is what we have learned for ourselves or been taught by the spirit.

There are all kinds of questions to be pondered, about who and what is represented by the golden-winged bird and the mysterious Aphoenicius with the shining eyes.

Each message, each lesson, each meaning, is tied into the deeper substance of serendipity. The fable may mean even more when you read it again—especially *after* this book's discussion of spiritual serendipity.

Part 4

Mental
Serendipity

Serendip

At the transition

to the twenty-first century

Serendipity Today

Now that we know a little about serendipity's past, it is time to move to the present. What is serendipity *today?* How does it work *now?* What is its relevance to *you?*

All good explanations involve definitions of terms and stories or experiences to illustrate. So we will begin there, and then move to some practical suggestions on how to gain the quality—and how to use it.

We begin with the kind of serendipity that is both generated and received by the mind, and by the five senses that the mind commands. This first level we will call "mental serendipity."

Definition of Terms
(the Words That Define the Word)

Serendipity, according to *Webster's* is "the making of pleasant discoveries by accident, the knack of doing this." Walpole would not have been completely satisfied with Webster's definition! After reading "The Three Princes" he wanted a word that meant more than "luck" or "accident." He wanted a word that celebrated life's sometimes happy unpredictability, but he also wanted a word that had to do with quality of life, a word that recognized the fact that "luck" comes most frequently to those who are aware, concerned, and wise. He created a word, a noun with an adjective form, that to him represented the universal meaning contained in the experiences of the princes of Serendip. "Serendipity" was defined by Walpole as *a quality of mind which, through awareness, sagacity and good fortune, allows one to frequently discover something good while seeking something else.*

Serendipitous is the adjective form. A serendipitous experience is one of unexpected happy discovery, and a serendipitous person is one who makes such discoveries frequently.

Quality of life refers to the joy and fulfillment level of our everyday living. It does not result from material possessions or external lifestyle. A significant and noticeable increase in quality of life results from the conscious development of a particular temperament of the soul which this book calls serendipity.

The *sensual awareness* that serendipity requires can be defined as alertness and effective *use* of the five senses. Each of our senses can be developed—fine-tuned so they present us with more beauty as well as more information, more opportunities and insight as well as more data. When we concentrate *only* on the task at hand, on the schedule, routine, or plan of the day, we are like the plowhorse with blinders on who sees only the straight furrow ahead of him. But when we focus on what is happening as well as on what we are doing—and on what is around us and in us—we begin to see ourselves as part of a far bigger picture and begin to be as aware of the feelings in our hearts as we are of the plans in our minds.

Mental awareness, another serendipity prerequisite, refers to both our education *and* our insights—our accumulated understanding and perspective as well as our alertness and vigilance, and our ability to be in the world and aware of the world in the most positive sense (which does not require us to be "of the world").

Sagacity, says *Webster's*, is "wisdom in one's understanding and judgment of things; insight springing both from education and from alertness." Sagacity, then, requires us to be both informed and aware; alert, sensitive, and empathetic. Just as it has been said that luck favors the prepared, it could be said that serendipity favors the sagacious and the aware.

Good fortune, says *Webster's*, is "luck; good things that happen without work or effort." Walpole wouldn't have wanted his word too closely associated with luck or lack of effort. He thought that serendipity could be obtained in greater frequency by *developing* both sagacity and good fortune. In his mind, then, good fortune was an *attitude* of faith and optimism—an attitude allowing one to see the bright, opportunistic side of unexpected occurrences—a love and an appreciation for surprises rather than a resentment of them.

Indeed, it is possible to *expect* the unexpected, to admit that life is unpredictable and that we control only a very small number of the variables, and then to *decide* to look for the positive interpretation, or "bright side," of everything that happens. This, in Walpole's mind, would constitute the *attitude* of good fortune.

Goals can be defined as "mental pictures of things as we want them to be." Goals are an essential part of serendipity. The fourth requirement set forth by Walpole, after awareness, sagacity, and good fortune, was to be "seeking something." Serendipity happens when we discover something good *while seeking something else*.

It is when we couple awareness and sagacity with purpose and goals that we create the atmosphere and attitudes within which serendipity can flourish.

While serendipity is helped by goals and direction, it is *hindered* by the heavy, overstructured plans and highly detailed lists and schedules that absorb all of our awareness, sucking us away from the opportunities and surprises of the *present*.

Double Exposure

Two competing images superimposed
atop each other
each partially observed, partially obscured,
so that
neither is vivid nor fulfilling.
Like twice-exposed film
our overprocessed plans split
our mind's capacity
between what we've planned and what is.
The picture of all our artificial schemes and
the tight, time-managed lists of what we think
we want to happen
is double-exposed over
the real-life adventure of what *is* happening.
Thus, so much of the irreplaceable present
is unobserved.
Beauties, ideas, opportunities, needs, humor,
and all kinds of
unplannable *feelings*
float by us in the periphery
of our blinder-shaded eyes.

Bridges

Serendipity is a bridge. The metaphor applies
in many ways. The first application is that
serendipity is a bridge between structure and
spontaneity, between discipline and flexibility,

between the expected and the unexpected, between plans and surprises, between relationships and achievements, and between the
forced and the fun. The second broad application applies to spiritual serendipity and will be
explained in the second part of this book.

Serendipity can be thought of as a sort of
bridge between metaphorical regions that are
otherwise hostile to each other—lands that,
without the "serendipity bridge," we have to
choose between because the gap separating
them is so wide.

One is the land of structure and discipline, of
goal setting, positive mental attitude, and
achievement. It is inhabited mainly by high-
powered business executives, aspiring yuppies,
left-brain thinkers, and superachievers. The
other is the land of spontaneity and flexibility,
of sensitivity, observation, and relationships.
Here we find many artists and creative thinkers, philosophers and would-be Renaissance
men, and people who use the intuitive right
hemisphere of their brains.

People in one land travel in jet planes, power
yachts, and snowmobiles. In the other land,
many prefer hot-air balloons, sailboats, and
cross-country skis.

Although there are overlaps, we generally as-
sociate people in each land with certain things:
In the first land, people read *The Wall Street
Journal*, dress for success, and listen to motiva-

tional tapes. In the second land, people read poetry, dress for comfort, and listen to Stravinsky. In land A politics means power, progress, military strength, and tax loopholes. In land B politics means environmental conservation, peace marches, and government welfare. In one land people live to work and say things like, "Act, don't react," and "Don't just sit there, do something." In the other land, people work to live and say things like, "Go with the flow" and "Don't just do something, sit there."

The problem most of us have is that we like a lot of things about both lands . . . and we like lots of the people in both lands. And there are certain parts of us that we know belong in each land. We recognize that each of the two places has its own unique beauty and usefulness. We also know that we appreciate one all the more after we have spent time in the other—like going from the snows of Colorado to a beach in California.

It is serendipity that allows us to get from one to the other, to spend time in both places, even to have a home in each land.

Remember that serendipity requires *sensitivity* and highly tuned observation so that we don't miss things like unexpected beauty, needs, opportunities, new ideas, and spontaneous moments. If we have this sensitivity and if we have clear goals and objectives (because serendipity only "finds something good" when "seeking something else"), then we have the passport and the visa that allows us to move freely between the two places.

With serendipity we can live comfortably in land A because we are "seeking things"—we have goals; we want to achieve, to grow, to progress. But we can also feel at home in land B because we have sensitivity and sagacity and are, therefore, flexible and spontaneous enough to change our minds and change our course when the right moment or the right need or the right surprise comes into view.

Serendipity is not only a bridge between places, it is a bridge between people—and between the two extremes that are sometimes painfully evident in our world. One extreme leans too far left, one too far right.

To illustrate, ponder two people (we'll call them Robert and Bob) with opposite approaches and attitudes. Robert is clean-cut and scrubbed. He's always in coat and tie. He sets goals with precision and regularity. He plans his weeks and his days. He is extremely conservative politically. His heroes, other than Rush Limbaugh and Pat Robertson, are Milton Friedman, Barry Goldwater, and Ronald Reagan, as well as various corporate CEOs and captains of industry. He is a high achiever. He is meticulous in his use of his huge day-timer. He drives a new car. He is financially well off

but wants to be rich. He believes in free enter-
prise, personal responsibility, and progress. He
sees technology as having most of the answers
for our physical future and has little patience
with conservationists who want to stop progress in order to cling to the past. He believes
that uncompromised obedience is the central
doctrine of God and dislikes people who want
to know the reasons for everything.

Bob feels uncomfortable in ties, wears
mostly jeans and soft shoes, likes his hair long.
His favorite presidents were Kennedy and
F.D.R. He sees himself as a social liberal, gets
involved in inner-city projects, and feels a
strong obligation to help minorities and equal-
ize society. He prides himself on spontaneity
and dislikes a lot of structure and routine in his
life. He likes natural things and organic foods,
does a lot of hiking and camping, thinks pre-
serving the environment should be a higher
priority than building another refinery. He
seems unconcerned about money and material
things. He believes there is a lot to learn from
Eastern thought, particularly meditation and
"flowing with the current of life rather than always trying to swim upstream." He believes
that tolerance and compassion is the heart of
true religion and feels that truth is learned
largely through questioning and even sometimes through doubting . . . until it can be
sorted out.

If you were to ask Robert to compare himself
with Bob, he would do so like this:

Me: Winner, clean, proactive, goal setter and
planner, freedom, progress, modern, believing.
Him: Loser, dirty, reactionary, aimless, so-
cialistic, backward, out-of-date, doubting.

On the other hand, if you asked Bob to compare himself to Robert, he would do so like this:

Me: Friendly, compassionate, real, natural,
thoughtful, love for earth, comfortable, practical, no class structure, independent thinking.
Him: Pushy, selfish, artificial, arbitrary,
exploitive, stuffed shirt, class- and prestige-
oriented, close-minded, blind faith.

Because of their extremes, both Robert and
Bob seem more wrong than right. Each has
disconnected himself from an important half of
life. Each needs the bridge.

Not only can people who have built the bridge
of serendipity have the best of both worlds,
they can *become* the best of both. They can be
the good parts of Robert and Bob and avoid the
dangerous extremes of each. They can derive
joy from giving and from getting. They can find
real fulfillment in meeting a goal, in checking
off things on their to-do list, in competing, and
in winning. But they can also feel the joy of

a red sunset, of doing a spur-of-the-moment anonymous good turn, of writing a poem, or of winning a small smile from a small child.

Serendipity is a *bridge* that lets us have our cake and eat it too. We don't have to choose between being structured schedulers or flexible free-lancers. We can have both goals *and* surprises, both plans *and* spontaneity, both discipline *and* flexibility. We can ride in jet planes *and* hot-air balloons. We can get there *and* enjoy the journey.

A Curious, Calm Capacity

Academic, analytical, or anecdotal definitions
of "serendipity"
are fine up to a point. But they don't define
feeling;
and serendipity is a feeling
that most of us know,
whether we've ever called it by the word
or not.
It is the feeling of those rare days
when everything works,
when, without apparent effort,
things just seem to fall into place. . . .

When we're having one of those days . . .
when we've got it,
we know it!
But we can only partially define or describe it,

this subtle sense, so seldom secured,
so soft, so simple, a subtle slowing of time . . .
so that there is enough for beauty,
for love, for people;
and inner peace enough
to look into people's eyes with interest
instead of self-consciousness.
Time to wait for some things to come to you
rather than going after them;
unpressured, uncompetitive, yet confident.

The curious, calm capacity to enjoy simply,
to think freely, to feel deeply,
to observe others
instead of worrying about their observations
of you.

A soft stillness inside, feeling the ground
through shoe soles and the sky all around.
In this mood, surprises come—
unplanned, unexpected,
even unhoped for things—
better than what we planned,
fuller than what we hoped,
and far more interesting.
Surprise and delight,
the world seems open to us, and filled with
unanticipated beauty.
People cease to be threats, bores, irritations,
or interruptions
and become at least interesting,

at best fascinating . . .
and able to provide, somehow, what we need—
even more in fact
than what we knew we needed.

Application of
the Attitude

Structure or Spontaneity

Imagine a carefully planned trip:

Goal: A working vacation,
            specific objectives
            for accomplishing things *and*
            for having fun.

Plan: Very detailed.
            Every minute planned,
            guidebooks read, lists of
            things to see, time allotted,
            where to stay, eat, stop, start,
            appointments set,
            all on paper, all structured.

Results: Some goals met but a lot of:
            ☐ Irritation (delays, foul-ups,
            "the best laid plans . . .")
            ☐ Disappointment (most things
            not as good as their billings)
            ☐ Opportunities missed (wasn't
            looking for them—not on list)

☐ Beauty missed (didn't notice it—unmentioned in guidebook)
☐ Relationships missed (no time for people without appointments)
☐ Fatigue (it's exhausting when you have to force everything)
☐ Offense (*given* by irritation, *taken* through impatience)
☐ Unwelcome surprises (unanticipated things always interrupting)
☐ Stress (feeling the need to get home and rest)

Resolution: Next time plan better, read better guidebook.

Now imagine the opposite—a trip taken on a whim:

Goal: Relax
Plan: None
Result: Some nice moments but a lot of:
☐ Frustrations (reservations needed, people unavailable)
☐ Wasted time (places not open, keep getting lost)
☐ Restlessness (should really be *accomplishing* something)
☐ Boredom (not much happening)
☐ Stress (wanting to get home where there is control)

Resolution: Next time stay home . . . it's

> easier to relax
> in familiar surroundings.

Now picture the combination—the serendipity journey:

Goal: Business and pleasure: "get there" and "enjoy the journey."

Plan: Priorities and necessities planned but much room consciously left for flexibility and spontaneity (an *attitude* adventure).

Results: ☐ Objectives met (sometimes upgraded, exceeded)
             ☐ Discoveries (often of things better than what was sought)
             ☐ Surprises (of beauty, of interest, of new ideas)
             ☐ Friends found (new acquaintances—common interests)
             ☐ Needs noticed (chances to help, teach, give)

Resolution: Keep traveling!

My Epiphany

As a college student, I developed a "positive mental attitude," set a dozen or so specific goals every week, and planned every minute of every day and most of every night. I set high goals, made detailed plans, and attempted to shut out anything that fell outside of my plans. I tried hard to force life to work out the way I wanted it, and to reach my own objectives even if I had to step on a few people to do so. Since I saw only what I wanted to see, I was quite happy . . . until finally someone (it happened to be a girl I was dating) pointed out that I was insensitive, self-centered, rigidly structured, obsessed, and selfish, not to mention unspon-taneous and un-fun.

By sheer coincidence (or maybe by unde-served serendipity) our last date (the one on which she unloaded) was to a concert given by the *Serendipity Singers*. I had no idea what the word meant, but the next day, sitting in the li-brary and still reeling from my chastisement, I happened to look the word up in the huge, unabridged library dictionary. The defi-nition fascinated me. "The ability, through sagacity, sensitivity, and spontaneity, to find something good while looking for something else." An *ability*, the dictionary called it. Was this the quality by which one could have the left-brain goals and plans of an achiever *and* the right-brain flexibility and sensitivity of an artist? I began to see the concept as a *bridge* between the objectives, structure, and high achievement pattern (which I'd worked hard on and wasn't about to give up) and the fun, flexibility, and lightheartedness that I had ap-parently lost.

I made the word my motto.

Serendipity is not a compromise or midpoint between structure and spontaneity. It is an ability, a capacity, and a frame of mind that lets a person have more of *both* than he could have of *either*. Setting goals, with an accompanying determination to stay flexible and to keep *looking* for something better reveals shortcuts to the goals one has set as often as it reveals better destinations.

Origins and Results

Mental serendipity involves intense use of the five senses and yields greater beauty observed, adventure, and more pleasure and joy through what eyes see, ears hear, senses sense. Serendipity trains both of the brain's hemispheres to gather and to value knowledge and results in understanding, joyous openings of truth and insight—and eventually, true wisdom.

The *sources* as well as the *benefits* of serendipity can also be social and emotional.

Social serendipity allows us to see all people as interesting, helps us watch for chance meetings, chances to learn, chances to give, and puts into our hands the joystick of friends everywhere, even in places we've never been.

Emotional serendipity lets us become fascinated with (rather than resentful of) our own moods. We *observe* our depression, our pensiveness, even our fear—and find within them insight and depth.

In all cases, serendipity involves a certain combination of awareness, observation, acceptance, and optimism that lets us find the best in whoever we are with, whatever is going on, wherever we are, wherever we are living, and however we are feeling. In all cases we are *finding and flowing* instead of *forcing and fighting*.

Scientists, explorers, and inventors tell us their key discoveries often come in one of two ways:

1. In solitary periods of private, penetrating, almost painful thought
2. In bursts of insight that come not out of analysis but out of observation or incidental conversation—or simply out of nowhere (from some source beyond)

It is the same with *our* discoveries, about ourselves and about life. They come to us either through deep, free thought or through observation and awareness—all of which are destroyed by trying to control everything, by excessive and exaggerated "positive mental attitude," by forcing the issue, by frantic activity, and by planning every minute.

For many years, our society has recognized the need for *balance* in life—for prioritizing and taking care of things that really matter. While we talk more and more about the *problem* of balance, we keep getting offered the same tired old "cures" of positive mental attitude and time management. So many people carry both to excess. Positive mental attitude starts to mean "ignoring reality and trying to force everything to be as I want it" and time management begins to suggest "making longer and longer lists and trying to do more and more things."

Serendipity is an alternative attitude. It does involve being positive and having goals, but it *also* involves flexibility, spontaneity, sensitivity, and the relish of surprise.

All of this brings us to our first formula, our first equation for serendipity, our first motto. In longhand it would be "Live with acute awareness and steady sagacity and ponder deeply life's goals and destinations." In shorthand, *Watch and think.*

The Source
(You)

An Umbrella and a Lens

Whence cometh serendipity?
From ourselves!
It is a quality and a gift
that can be given only by ourselves

and only to ourselves.
We give it by teaching ourselves to
watch and think,
to look for beauty, ideas, relationships,
to relish the unexpected . . .
to welcome surprises as opportunities,
even if they delay or alter
(and sometimes replace)
the goals we have thoughtfully set and
pursued.

Mental serendipity
is a translucent, rose-colored
umbrella
that overarches
our physical, mental, social, and
emotional lives,
making them dynamic, and allowing each part
of us
to see happily through rain or shine.

And serendipity is an infrared, wide-angle lens
that lets us see more
and see each part clear, and bright, and light,
even in night.

The development of serendipity
is not merely a mental process
(like learning a new memory technique)
or a physical process
(like muscle conditioning).

Rather, it is an attitude
of thoughtfulness and watchfulness
that changes how we see the world
and how we want to live in it.

The Process
(of gaining the quality)

"Exercises"

To go into training for a race, one sets up a regimen of regular exercise and disciplined habits.
To become watchful and thoughtful enough to
summon serendipity we need training exercises
or habits that attract the quality. Nine exercises
follow—but first a story to refocus the *nature*
of serendipity.

While I was living and working in London,
the president of our organization flew in from
the U.S. headquarters. I was asked to meet his
plane and take him to his hotel. The late flight
arrived at the end of a long Heathrow concourse in the still of the night. The president,
an elderly man, was tired and jet-lagged, yet I
saw in his eyes, his words, and his handshake,
an awareness, a concern.

Walking down the concourse with him and
his personal assistant, a man named Arthur, I
noticed that his briefcase had a broken hasp

and sagged open. I walked a half step behind, ready to retrieve anything that might fall out. Then his assistant noticed the problem and took action, dramatically pulling off his belt and fastening it around the briefcase. The president watched, with a twinkle in his eye, and said, "Thank you, Arthur, but are you sure we don't now have a more serious problem?"

As we proceeded toward the airport exit I noticed how aware he was—how interested in the environment and the people that passed. Repeatedly he caught someone's eyes and nodded a greeting.

Finally we emerged to the waiting chauffeur-driven Rolls-Royce, a huge, long limousine I had hired in an attempt to increase his comfort and signify the respect of those of us who ran the British office. I worried now that he would think it pretentious and out of place, but he climbed in without a word. As we drove down the dark motorway toward London, he stirred, stood, walked up to the front seat, and put his hand on the shoulder of the professional chauffeur who came with the car. "Young man," the president said, "it's very late and I'm sorry if we are keeping you away from your family this evening."

This wise leader didn't focus on the majestic car, or on hurrying to his hotel, or on his own fatigue. What he saw were the needs, the people, the opportunities, and even the humor of the evening. None of what he said or did was planned or scheduled; all was an outgrowth of who he was and what he noticed.

How do we train ourselves to see with that sensitivity and that serendipity. Here are nine answers (some may sound strange—until we're reminded that the aim is to help us *watch* . . . and *think*):

1 Write Poetry

You have to see something rather clearly
to write poetry about it.
Further, you have to see with some insight,
or involvement, or irony
and to *feel* something in what you see.
Writing poetry (even attempting) forces one
to notice, and to think, and to feel.
Worrying about the poem's quality or your ability
is mute,
because the readership is *you*.

2 Slow
  Down

Consciously walk a little slower, *move* a little
slower.
Hurry tramples watchfulness
and thoughtfulness.
Smell the flowers, feel the sun, pause to
breathe.
Notice the needs of others
and try to feel empathy.
Sometimes relaxing your pace
can lengthen your stride.

3 Welcome
  Surprises

And anticipate them, look for them,
expect them,
relish them.
Surprises, well received, don't
knock you off course.

They reveal new destinations
and new directions.

4 Enjoy the Journey—Now

"Are we having fun yet?"
says the popular T-shirt message.
Thinking of the happiness
and fulfillment of life
as a misplaced thing, likely to be found later,
after you "get there,"
is living in a low realm of high folly.
Look for (and find) joy today.
Notice the moments,
Remember that life is not a dress rehearsal.

5 Hold "Sunday Sessions"

Spend a half hour alone,
on the first day of the week,

looking ahead to the other six, and
thinking about
what matters, about priorities and
opportunities.
Without goals, serendipity won't work.
We need the "else" if we want to
"find something of value while
seeking something else."
Regular Sunday sessions *adjust* and *refine* goals
as new options appear and new capacities grow.

6 Simplify and Set
Your Own Standards

The trading of time for things is usually a
bad deal.
When the *things* are the expensive trappings
of style,
image, and impression,
the trade-off can be a disaster.
Advertising is the fine art
of trying to make us think
we need
what we actually only want.
And trying to impress others with the newest

and costliest
car, fashion, brand name, address, toy, or trend
is the depth of bad-deal trade-offs
and the height of self-deceit.

7 Make Goals Without Plans

While goals are an indispensable part of
serendipity,
tight, over-detailed plans are *not*.
Spend your Sunday Session and other
"thought time"
conceptualizing your goals, visualizing them,
and laying out a general route toward them,
but acknowledge that your actual path
will be some combination of the schedule
and the surprise.

8 Set Up Split-Page
Scheduling

If you're a list maker
make your list (or write your schedule)
on the left side of your page.
Draw a line down the center
and leave the right side blank until day's end.
Then, there on the right,
jot down the day's serendipity
(think back, remember
a new acquaintance, a fresh idea,
a child's question,
an unexpected opportunity, a friend's need,
a chance meeting, a beautiful flower).
For fun, at the end of the week,
look back on the lefts and rights of your days
and discover
that what "just happened" on the
unknown right
is often more valuable than
what you made happen on the known left.
If you are already committed
to a particular type
of schedule book or planner,
stay with it, but alter it by putting a vertical
"serendipity line"

down the center of every page.
Keep your structure to the left,
your spontaneity to the right.
If you are free of present commitments
to a particular type of planner,
try the monthly "anti-planner"
mentioned at the end of this book.

9 Have Faith—Believe in Serendipity

"Nothing is coincidence,"
says Redfield in *The Celestine Prophecy.*
Believe it.
There is something cosmic that connects
everything.
When we believe in the connections we begin
to see them.
When you miss a flight, maybe there is
someone you should meet on the next one.
Have faith that things happen for a reason,
that there is opportunity (and beauty)
in everything.
We attract serendipity by believing in it.

"Life as Experience" and "Goals Without Plans"

Too much planning can make the actual experience of living almost anticlimactic. (There may be times for reading the script, but it's never as exciting as ad-libbing.)

Too much *thinking about* something removes us from it—we become observers, analysts, spectators, or critics rather than participants.

If we can approach life more as an *experience* that contains vast variety and infinite potential for surprise, we will find ourselves dealing less with success and failure and more with progress and growth.

If we have to think about every detail of our lives, we ought to sometimes think about them *after* they have been lived (when we can learn from experience), not always *before* (when the very thought may intercept or alter the experience). The best time to be aware of details is not before or after, but *now*. Approaching life as an experience makes us, moment to moment, more aware of what is happening and of what we *are* feeling—and less aware of what we planned to have happen or wish *had* happened. Thus we see the opportunities we could never have planned and realize far more serendipity than we otherwise could.

It is not goals that get in the way of experience or serendipity—it is inflexible plans.

Goals can coexist with real-time experience—they can shine like beacons and allow us to see our experiences more clearly and more in the light of what we could learn from them or make of them. Know well the destination of a goal, but use the serendipity of a compass to get there, not the rigidity of a road map.

Summary

Walpole, whether he knew it or not, told us *how* to get mental serendipity in his definition of the word.

"The ability," he said, "through *sagacity* and *good fortune* to find something good while *looking for* something else."

Three requirements:

1. *Sagacity:* Notice, watch, observe, be aware, learn, refuse to wear the blinders of obsession or self-consciousness.

2. The attitude of *good fortune:* See changes as opportunities, surprises as excitement, disappointments with silver linings.

3. Thoughtful *goals:* Set and list objectives and pursue them until something else (better) is discovered.

And while Walpole did not profess to be a spiritual man or to have coined a spiritual word, serendipity, even as he defined it, is at least partially a quality of the spirit because it is only with the "deeper eyes" of the spirit that we really see and become truly sagacious.

But there is a level of serendipity beyond the concept that Walpole conceived. It is not coincidentally but *purposefully* spiritual. We will get to it after a brief intermission.

i n t e r m i s s i o n

I've taken to putting intermissions
in my books
for the same reason they occur in stage plays:
to give the audience a chance to stretch
and to ponder the plot
before it thickens.
This book has a particular need
for a break and a breather—
because at this point, we change *levels*.
The serendipity we turn to now
is a quality of the soul
rather than of the mind.
Our sources shift from senses to spirit,
and our attitude from flexibility to faith.
Even the underlying question changes from
"What do I want, and how can I find it?"
to
"What does God want for me,
and how can I receive it?"

In the book *Lifebalance* (coauthored with my
wife, Linda), there is a section on balancing
structure and discipline with spontaneity and
flexibility. In it, we introduced serendipity as

the bridge between the two and presented concepts like split-page planning to encourage readers to cultivate and value unexpected opportunities and spur-of-the-moment impressions or ideas. During the writing of *Lifebalance* there came many moments when we wished to say things about serendipity that were inexpressible in secular wording. It was during that time that I realized that my definition now went far beyond Walpole's and that I had begun to think of the word as a spiritual term.

I realized that the most profound moments of serendipity in my own life—the times when I had truly discovered something of great value while seeking something else—had resulted from spiritual promptings. I realized that the awareness needed to trigger the most valuable kind of serendipity comes not from any of the five senses but from the far higher and far deeper "sixth sense" of the spirit.

If Walpole could invent a word, I decided, then I could certainly modify it and expand its meaning. From that moment, "spiritual serendipity" became part of my inner vocabulary and the quality to which I most aspired.

The problem with writing *this* book is that I don't know just where readers are as they read—how far along they are with life and with thinking about life. It took me decades to get to here. If I had read this book twenty years ago, I'm not sure I would have "got it." I was still into positive attitude, time-management, self-help, getting more done, ownership, accumulation, *control*. "Work and plan" would have meant more to me—much more—than "watch and think."

But times are changing. I'm certain that far more people are ready for serendipity today than were ready twenty years ago. There is a yearning for peace, for harmony, for commitments, for a slower yet more purposeful pace.

If you've come this far into the book and you're feeling like it's a bit too ethereal—if you're waiting for the car chase, the special effects, the three easy ways to get rich quick . . . you might want to set it aside. Come back to it in a few years when you feel the need for a higher source of help and when your heart starts telling you that maybe quality matters more than quantity, peace more than power, character more than control, and family more than fortune.

One other quick intermission comment:

Please keep in mind that this book is about an *attitude*. Forgetting what it is about can lead to misunderstandings.

One friend, very much into New Age and eastern philosophy and religion, read one portion of an early draft of this book and exclaimed, "This sounds like Buddhism—all this business about meditation and slowing down and being aware of what's inside of you."

Another friend, a Christian and equally candid, who read a different portion said, "You're
just talking about the Holy Spirit but using
some new terminology."

In fact, the book is not about the Holy Spirit
or the ideals and gospel of Christ, but it is
about an *attitude* of our spirits (actually of our
souls) that can make us more receptive to both.

And its objective is not the blissful *detach-
ment* of Buddhism, but the deeply *involved*
awareness and experience of serendipity.

Incidentally, I'm happy to say that both
friends understood much better after reading
the entire book.

Sit back down now.
The lights are blinking, and it's time
for the second act,
the second level of serendipity.

Part 5

Spiritual
Serendipity

Our world

At a time of spiritual transition

Serendipity of the Spirit

Even though it is best understood after understanding mental serendipity (and best applied
by one who has learned to apply mental
serendipity), *spiritual* serendipity is something
completely different—a separate and higher
form—different not only in degree but in kind.

With mental serendipity, our sagacity comes
through the awareness of our *senses*, through
the light and insight of our own feelings, and
from the wisdom of experience and education.

With spiritual serendipity, our sagacity comes
through the awareness of our *spirit*, through the
light of inspiration, and from the wisdom of God.

Just as the quality itself is higher, so is the
method and process of pursuit higher—and
harder. But it is worth all the effort we can give,
because the rewards of spiritual serendipity are
peace as well as power and serenity as well as
success.

Definition of Terms
(Higher Words for a Higher Quality)

Our spirit: The "hand within the glove." The
essence of who we are . . . which continues

after the body dies. The part of us that comes from God, that can communicate with God, that can return to God.

The Spirit: The light and power and influence that comes from a higher source—from God. (The name one gives God or the denominational religion, if any, that one follows matters less in the application of spiritual serendipity than the acknowledgment that God's spirit can guide ours and the commitment to both seek and follow that guidance.)

Gift: While mental serendipity is a gift from ourselves, spiritual serendipity is a gift from God. Since it relies on powers and perceptions beyond our own, it can be given only by that higher power. Still, it is *we* who determine whether we obtain the gift, because it is freely given to all who desire it and do what it requires.

Gifts: Each individual is unique—particularly in terms of his inherent talents and aptitudes, or "gifts." Gifts can be of a spiritual as well as a physical or mental nature and can include varied kinds of receptivity to nudges and inspiration.

Sixth sense: Thoughtful individuals recognize that the five senses are not their only source of knowledge or information. We can tune in to promptings, impressions, and insights. Our sixth (and far most valuable) sense consists of the feelings of our spirits.

Nudges or promptings: Impressions that come to our minds via our spirits and from The Spirit.

Tuning in: Like a faint radio signal, nudges can be tuned in and amplified until they become clear and spiritually audible.

Inspiration: A more direct term describing the impressions and guidance that can come from the mind of God to the mind of man.

Ask: We are given (both as a privilege and as an admonition) the opportunity to ask God for personal guidance. Asking, because of the power it connects us to, should be undertaken soberly and cautiously, and with a commitment to acquiescence and submission to God's will and wisdom.

Confirmation: Most believers, regardless of creed or denomination, agree that God's answers usually come not in detailed instruction but in directional promptings or in *feelings* of light or calmness or clarity that *confirm* our own directions or inclinations when they are right. When they have made a wrong decision, those who are receptive and spiritually in tune get the opposite feeling (confusion, murky hesitation). God seems to want us to sort things out the best we can and then bring our answer to him for confirmation—like a wise father who says, "I won't do your homework for you but I'll check and correct it with you after you do the work." Confirmation is the light, warm, calm, sure feeling by which we know our decision is right. Absence of that feeling is the dark stupor of thought that tells us we must work through the decision again.

Spiritual serendipity: That quality or gift which, through sagacity of both senses and spirit, and through the grace of God, allows one to ask for and receive guidance (inspiration and confirmation) relative to his purpose, his family, his service toward others, and his day-to-day activities.

Light and Guidance

As with mental serendipity,
spiritual serendipity cannot be completely defined
with words
(because, more than a word, it is a feeling).
Words are useful in attempting definition only
if they generate some image or glimpse
of the feeling.
Spiritual serendipity is the soft,
sweet submission
of spirit to
a conscious, welcome dependency on God.

Within spiritual serendipity is the
righteous, rigorous realization of the fact
that when it comes to long-range planning,
life is too complex for our own calculations.

Thus the goal of a guided life—guided
by a higher (indeed, highest) intelligence.

Spiritual serendipity is sunshine
that lights and reveals parts of the
landscape of the future
that would otherwise be dark and unnoticed.
This higher perspective brings calm, peace,
clarity.
It slows time down, enhances beauty,
and makes love, empathy, and sensitivity
more natural.
It is the influence
of a higher, wiser, stronger Spirit on our own.
This Spirit gives life and light to the body,
and transmits to and affects our every part.

*One hundred and fifty years ago, a man named
Parley Pratt spoke of a spiritual force that adapts itself to all our organs or attributes; quickens all the
intellectual faculties; increases, enlarges, expands,
and purifies all the natural passions and affections. . . . It inspires, develops, cultivates, and ma-
tures all the fine-tone sympathies, joys, tastes,
kindred feelings, and affections of our nature. It inspires virtue, kindness, goodness, tenderness, gentle-
ness, and charity. It develops beauty of person, form,
and features. It tends to health, vigor, animation,
and social feeling. It invigorates all the faculties of
the physical and intellectual man. It strengthens
and gives tone to the nerves . . . it is . . . joy to the*

heart, light to the eyes, music to the ears, and life to the whole being.*

Pratt also compared the spirit with electricity,
explaining how it could warm and light
those who, as pure conductors,
let it enter them.

The metaphor of electricity
(dramatic then because electricity was so new)
is perhaps even more accurate
now that electricity is
everywhere present
and always at our disposal.

The spiritual circuitry,
into which we can "plug" ourselves,
is always there, always available, always
complete.
No new line ever has to be jerry-rigged to
answer
our asking
or meet our needs.

We simply must understand how to plug in.
When we do, the world, along with ourselves,
is transformed.

The power of God's spirit, transmittable to
ours,

*Parley P. Pratt, *Key to Theology*, Deseret Book Co., 1965.

is so vast.
And its vastness alone, like a slow, sweeping
river
turning a waterwheel generator
makes it peaceful and calm, easy while strong.

We plug in with a three-prong plug
of awareness:
First, a prong of *sensual awareness*
that reveals opportunity, need, and deep
reality to us
through our five senses.
Second, a prong of *spiritual awareness*,
a knowing both of our own spiritual selves and
of a higher Spirit
together with an in-tuneness that pulls us to
prayer.
Third, a prong of *attitudinal awareness*
that allows us to *expect* discoveries of interest
and joy,
to savor the surprises of sense and of spirit.

It is this attitude, herein called
spiritual serendipity,
adopted into our souls,
that calms us, opens our vision,
and sweeps us into the currents of light.

We pursue serendipity of the spirit
by developing a deeper kind of awareness
that comes

through the senses,
through the spirit,
and through an attitude that values, cultivates,
and interconnects the two.

Many and varied writers and thinkers
(including M. Scott Peck in the single best-
selling modern book
of the last two decades*)
have concluded that a loving God must want us
to become more like Him.
It could be well argued that the
accumulation of additional awareness
is synonymous with progress
and that the difference between men and God,
vast as it is,
is essentially a difference in awareness.

We may be ready now for a clearer, simpler
definition
of spiritual serendipity.
It is the aware, submissive, and sensitive
condition of our spirits
which makes them susceptible
to the calm, the light, the peace, and the power
of God's spirit.

This higher serendipity
has the excitement and intrigue of a great *game*

The Road Less Traveled

in which we ask questions and make requests
and then try to summon the sensitivity
necessary
to recognize the answers
that come sometimes in disguise
and often with much stillness and subtlety.

Realizing the Ramifications

There is one last word to complete our "definition of terms." But before we get to it, pause for a moment to reflect on the overwhelming ramifications of this higher, more spiritual perspective. It is nothing less than a new way to view yourself, the people and circumstances around you, and the whole meaning of living here on this planet.

Once we have truly acknowledged that there is a higher intelligence, a higher power, a higher *being*—that He is interested in us and that His spirit can communicate with ours—everything should change, particularly our way of making choices, setting goals, and living from day to day.

Mental serendipity enhances our joy and expands our opportunities through better use of our own sensitivity and our own senses.

Spiritual sensitivity takes joy and opportunity to a different level by accessing parts of God's total awareness and insights. Like floodlights coming on in a stadium; like shifting into a higher, smoother, faster gear; like suddenly seeing through a window instead of into a mirror . . . we can feel differently, we can see better, we can be more.

Spiritual serendipity means abandoning the limiting oxymoron of self-help and turning to the liberating principle of faith, which is our final term to define. *Faith*, this paradigm-changing principle and spiritual-serendipity prerequisite, means three things:

1. A true, mind-changing *belief.* Substantial majorities profess belief in God. But real faith requires a realization of the powerful, personal implications of that belief. Faith means an acknowledgment of our own extremely limited perspective and potential and of the ultimate perspective and power of God. Faith means a grasping of the reality that He is there, that He is aware, that He cares, that He communicates. Faith means actual acceptance of His love and concern for us and real belief that His spirit can guide ours; that we can *feel* what is right; that there is a sixth sense (of spiritual feelings) that we can trust and rely on; that when our abilities and capacities run out, we can reach up and grab onto an ultimate capacity and power.

Many may have to pause and seriously reflect on this—and pray about it—before the balance of this book can have real effect. "Be still and know," the scripture says. Be still and think about feelings you've had that you know were right, about times when you've known you were more than a temporary mind and body, about times when you've felt (even fleetingly) something awesome, something bigger than yourself. Be still and know.

2. A *commitment* to seek God's guidance, and to strive to confirm our lives to it, even to submit and turn ourselves over to it. Beyond understanding there must be action. Beyond belief there must be commitment. Like anyone, God is more likely to give guidance that will be *followed*.

The whole notion of serendipity is "finding something good while seeking something else." The crux of faith and spiritual serendipity is trusting that what God will guide us to (if we ask, if we seek, if we see) will be better than what we could find for ourselves.

3. The *mental effort* of asking for and receiving guidance, of watching for and finding answers, and of visualizing something the way it could be, mentally seeing what has to happen to bring it to pass and then applying your power and prayer's power to do it.

It has been said, "When we work by faith, we work by mental and spiritual effort rather than by physical force."

The Second Bridge

While mental serendipity can make a bridge between our structured and spontaneous selves, spiritual serendipity can be the span between our goals and God's will, between our limited ability and perspective and His ultimate knowledge and power, between our finite senses and His infinite awareness.

The bridge of spiritual serendipity is essentially the application of faith to rise above ourselves and go beyond what we could be alone. This divine-girded bridge has unlimited span. It can give us the best of yin and yang, it can draw down power that connects and synergizes the otherwise opposites of aggressiveness and sensitivity, ambition and peace, confidence and humility.

Recall Robert and Bob (from page 104), the extremes on the right and left. What if each were asked about their spiritual views—particularly about their impressions of Jesus Christ—and the kind of example and model they thought He was? Robert's logic might go something like this: "Christ was the most *successful* being of all time. He had the objective of changing the world and He did it. He was totally disciplined, totally strong. He overcame the world. He taught people self-reliance and gave them confidence. His goal for us is eternal progress. Right and wrong were absolutes for

Him. He told us the path was straight and narrow and said He could not look on sin with the least degree of allowance. He expects us to stay on that path, and to remember that where much is given, much is expected. He exemplified self-discipline and taught that faith without works is dead."

Bob, on the other hand, would say: "Jesus Christ turned man's selfish and conceited beliefs upside down. He showed that real greatness is measured not by how many serve you but by how many you serve; not by what you get but what you give. The outer trappings of success meant nothing to Him. He was interested in the *inside* of people. Those He condemned were the 'successes,' the people who thought they had achieved. He cared about everyone, He gave to everyone, He wanted happiness for everyone. He taught us that people matter more than things. He taught us humility by letting us know that He was our salvation, that it was by His grace we are saved after all we can do."

Who is right? Robert or Bob?

Both are right.

Christ, particularly for Christians, but actually for anyone who studies His life and attitudes, can be thought of as the embodiment and the perfect example of *all* attributes—even those that we often think of as the antithesis of each other. Christ was not a compromise between good qualities. He was the epitome of all good qualities.

Consider briefly a list of qualities that we normally consider to be opposites, that usually stand opposed or in contrast to each other. Then realize that Christ exemplifies what is best about each side of each pair:

ambition	vs.	interest in "in-significant" persons
self-development	vs.	self-denial
masculine qualities (strength, power)	vs.	feminine qualities (tenderness, gentleness)
confidence	vs.	humility
conviction	vs.	sympathy
stern personal standards	vs.	tolerance
susceptibility to deep grief	vs.	boundless joy
commitment	vs.	patience and freedom from anxiety
calm compassion	vs.	righteous indignation

Lao Tzu, founder of Taoism, six hundred years before Christ, said, "If there ever comes a being who is both the yin and the yang, that being will not be a man, he will be God."

For Christians, Christ is that being. His ex-

ample expands our perspective and, for those
with faith, our potential. But the essence of all
great religions generates peace and purpose as
it *combines* all truth, and pulls all things together. True spirituality is the best of both
worlds. It is the ultimate *balance*. It teaches us
to pursue all of Robert's righteous qualities and
to overcome all of his self-righteous ones. It
teaches us to pursue all of Bob's sensitivities
and concerns and to cast aside any of his weak-
ness or lack of direction.

Spiritual serendipity, because it draws on
higher powers exemplified by Christ, can become a bridge between *all* good qualities, even
those we often see humanly personified as opposites.

The gospel of Christ
(or the true teachings of any great religion)
nourishes our spirituality and
draws us toward the best of both worlds, . . .
and promises,
if we are wise enough to learn and to follow,
that we can ultimately be partakers of
the best of *all* worlds.

A more pointed definition of faith
is "spirit-reliance,"
juxtapositioned against self-reliance.
Yet the two are not opposites.

One is a progression of the other.
We rely on self until we reach our limits,
then we bridge to spirit.

Imagine for a moment that God, our spiritual
father
made this earth
of options, opposites, obstacles
and opportunities
as a learning place for us
(mortality is a school and a test)
so that we could experience, grow,
become more of ourselves
and more like Him.
(The easiest things to imagine are things that
are true.)
Imagine that, like a college student away from
home
we learn self-reliance and independence here.
But access to home—guidance, support—
sustains us and unlimits us.

Faith, the bridge between what we can do
alone
and what God can do with us,
is the core of spiritual serendipity.
Alone, self-reliance wraps us in the small
package
of ourselves.
We burst through and billow beyond
with the spirit-reliance of faith.

With self-reliance alone we see
along the narrow shaft of our own
weak light,
a tunnel of dimness,
focused on a fabricated future,
passing through a present of
magnificent light.
Faith splits open our tunnel of limitation
and floods us with the beauty and possibility
of now.
Faith is about the future,
but it operates in and on the present.
It is an enhancing of the *awareness*
that is the core of serendipity.

"Today, well lived,"
said the Sanskrit poet,
"makes every yesterday a dream of joy
and every tomorrow a vision of hope."
Faith draws nudges, not blueprints.
God shows us the next step
but wants faith exercised again and again
before we see all that is at the top of the
staircase.
Thus He keeps us watching, looking, seeking
(unstagnant, unsatisfied, unasleep).
And He keeps us asking
and thus closer, more in contact
with Him.

The Higher Realm
(of Soul and Spirit)

One of the most fascinating (though perhaps least quoted and least understood) verses in the New Testament was mentioned briefly in the Overture. It comes from the fourth chapter of James, verses 13 and 14.

Go to now, ye that say, Today or tomorrow we will go into such a city, and continue there a year, and buy and sell, and get gain:
Whereas ye know not what shall be on the morrow. For what is your life? It is even a vapor, that appeareth for a little time, and then vanisheth away.

One remarkable thing about these verses is the *current* sound of their terminology. With minor adjustments they seem to translate into blunt criticisms of the self-help, pseudo-positive attitude and goal-setting salesmanship mentality of today. It could almost read:

Go on, you who say, Our plan calls for us to go into such and such a city tomorrow, and over a year's time we will meet the sales and profit quotas and accomplish our business plan:
Don't be so presumptuous. You can't plan or control very much of what will happen in the future. Who do

*you think you are? You are not of that much conse-
quence, and you won't even be around for very long.*

The scriptural advice that follows in the very
next verse of James is also as current and as important today as it was then:

*For that ye ought to say, If the Lord will, we shall
live, and do this, or that.*

The fact is, only God knows enough about
the circumstances of our future (or about our
abilities and gifts) to be able to tell us what we
should do and who we should be.

But is James (held by most scholars to be
Jesus' half brother—raised with Him in Mary
and Joseph's house) telling us not to set goals
or make plans? And is that what Jesus Himself
meant when He said, "Take no thought for the
morrow"?

Let's defer the question for a moment—long
enough to tell a story:

I was sitting in my management consulting
office one day late in autumn, writing a memo
to a client. The Sunday before, Linda and I, in
our traditional "Sunday session," or planning
time together, had looked at our long-range
goals and reviewed our commitments to certain things we wanted to do professionally over
the next five years.

The phone rang in the outer office and my

receptionist buzzed me. "A President Tanner on the phone for you," she said.

"What President Tanner?" I inquired. "President of what?" She said she didn't know, so I pushed the lit-up button on the phone and said, "Hello." (Luckily I didn't say the first thing that came to mind, which was the line from the movie *A Thousand Clowns* where Jason Robards says, "Hello, is this someone with good news or money?")

It was a secretary on the other end of the line who said, "Mr. Eyre, President Tanner would like to speak with you."

"Which President Tanner?" I asked again.

"*The* President Tanner," the voice said icily.

Suddenly I realized that it was Elder Tanner from the presidency of our church, calling from the world headquarters. I didn't know him personally and couldn't imagine why he would call.

After a greeting and some friendly questions about our family, he asked if Linda and I could come and see him the next day. Our church has a lay ministry where people are "called" to serve in various administrative positions—usually for relatively short periods of time but often at some personal and professional sacrifice—so we felt some apprehension when we entered his office the following day.

President Tanner, in his charming, gracious way, engaged us in pleasant small talk for a half hour (we becoming more curious and more *worried* every minute). Finally, amidst questions about family and general well-being, he popped the question: Would we be willing to leave our home and career for three years to go to southern England and supervise the church's affairs there?

In the brief time we spent thinking about it, it became obvious to us that if we really believed—and if we really wanted to put God's will above our own—we had to say yes to such a call. We did, and it was to become one of the greatest opportunities and experiences of our lives.

When we got back to our house after the meeting, we noticed our carefully calculated five-year goals still laying on the desk where we had worked on them the day before. We picked them up and realized that they had been completely superseded by our call. At that moment the verse from James echoed in my mind: "You know not what shall be on the morrow." Our five-year plans had vanished like vapor. I suppose the experience could be called serendipity because it was a happy surprise, and it transcended what we had planned. It was a *macro* level example of what happens all the time on the micro level. Spiritual serendipity is not usually a three-year calling. It's a small need, an unexpected opportunity, a flash of insight or idea,

a little impression to do or say something, or
an unexpected chance to deepen a relationship.

Ask and Answer

Was James discouraging goals and plans?
What did Christ mean when he said,
"Take no thought for the morrow"?
Was He speaking only to His apostles
or to those who receive some majestic calling
from God?
Is it only major events or spiritual epiphanies
that alter our aims, puncture our plans?
Or are there smaller things—little, subtle,
unexpected, impossible-to-anticipate
situations, events, occurrences
(and also feelings, promptings,
and impressions)
that enter our lives almost every day?
Of course there are!
We really *don't* know
what the morrow will hold!
The question is not
whether we can anticipate, predict,
and plan everything.
(We *can't*.)
The question is whether we will try to avoid,
ignore,
or push aside
things not of our making, things which don't
quite fit

with our plans.
We could have said no to the life-changing
three-year call
("No, thanks anyway, it doesn't fit into our
five-year goals."),
but to do so, we would have had to commit
the absurdity
of putting our objectives above God's.
So what about the smaller but similar day-to-
day absurdity
of pushing plans instead of following feelings—
feelings of the spirit which come as soft, silent,
inner suggestions
and which may be subtle, unexpected answers
to questions about what is best for ourselves
and for others . . . keys
to seeing beyond sight,
to the desires of our hearts,
to the questions of our prayers.

So back to the question we left hanging:
Is James telling us we are unwise
to set goals and make plans?
Is life a card game
with results based mainly on
the luck of the draw?
Or a chess game where we are pawns
moved by other's dominance
or by acts of God?
No.
But life might well be thought of

(by a believer in a personal God who cares
about us
and who can guide us)
as a different kind of game, a game of
Ask and answer.
We *ask* for insight and direction to know
His will. We ask in simple prayer
to know what is best for ourselves
and for others . . . to know beyond what we
can see. We ask in our own words.
And He *answers*—always—
but not always in the way or at the time
or the place
we expect.
The answers,
(always in God's language
of inspiration, impressions, feelings, and light)
may come quickly and directly to us as we ask
and analyze,
ponder and plan;
or they may come *later*,
in unexpected forms at unexpected moments.

These answers may be missed by those with
rigid plans
(because they may not acknowledge or even
notice
an answer
that fits outside of those plans).
Answers are also missed by those
without *any* goals

(because without some goals
or hopes or dreams
they cannot ask the right questions
nor have they *thought* enough to be able to
recognize
the answers when they come).

In this game the wise player *connects*
the answers that come
with the goals he has set
and with the questions he has asked.
The game is won by thinking hard
("mental effort")
about the right goals and the right questions
and *finding*
(or recognizing when they faintly appear)
the right answers.

Ask and answer is a difficult game
but an uncommonly rewarding one.
And the winners are the thinkers,
the observers,
the inquirers, and the listeners.
Think of it for a moment in terms of *realms:*
There is a low realm
in which people float, sometimes passive,
sometimes resentful,
letting the world push, mold, shove,
and shape them
as it will,
following the course of least resistance . . .

going nowhere, hurrying.
There is the middle realm
where people do their best to take control
of themselves and their destinies,
shaping events, setting goals,
making things happen,
drawing a blueprint and then building it.
There is a *higher* realm, higher than the low,
and higher than the middle.
It involves first:
Prayerfully, carefully setting goals,
asking, striving to have enough inspiration to
make them
conform to God's will.
(Sometimes God "gives us a light"
even as we pray.)
Second:
Watching for answers, further light and
knowledge,
nudges
that make our destiny, our foreordination, and
God's will
more clear . . . and then accepting them,
acting on them,
from moment to moment,
and changing our goals when necessary
to fit
the clearer view.

Better Than a Light

Sometimes God delays the light in order to allow us to develop faith, not answering at the moment we ask, but later, wanting us to be able to both wait and notice. The beauty of having faith to ask and to follow shines through the well-known verse:

I said to the man who stood at the gate of years
"Give me a light that I might step forth"
and the voice came back to me,
"Step out into the darkness
and put your hand in mine,
for that
is better than a light,
and surer than a known way."

It was suggested earlier that the key to mental serendipity is "Watch and Think." The corresponding methodology for spiritual serendipity is "Watch and Pray."

Watch and Pray

Answers come sometimes as we pray,
sometimes later as we watch.
This higher realm of guidance involves a
whole new
approach to life—
an approach where we prayerfully set

long- and short-range goals,
but continue to watch and pray for the added
insight
and the expanded opportunity that may lift
those goals
to higher and happier and healthier levels.
It is an approach that requires
frequent reevaluation, meditation, prayer,
and faith.

It is an approach exclusively available to those
who believe
in a personal God who can and will give
light,
and in the fact that we ourselves possess
far too little knowledge, far too narrow an
understanding
to adequately guide ourselves.

All who believe in these two things (God's
love and
our own inadequacy)
have the reason for wanting—
and the perspective required for gaining—
spiritual serendipity.

The Source
(the Spirit)

We have defined spiritual serendipity as
a feeling, a quality, an attitude, a condition of
our spirit
(calm, aware, peaceful, still, sure)
that makes us more receptive to *His* spirit.
The answers and insights we are looking for
are often already here—around us and
inside us—
although sometimes subtle, sometimes hidden.
Serendipity of our spirit lets us see them,
find them,
feel them.

God's spirit is the source of the serendipity
of our spirit.
Perhaps there are other *partial* sources:
Deep meditation may bring a certain stillness,
making us prone or susceptible
to unexpected discoveries about self and life.
And a slow, measurable alpha-state
brain wave pattern,
which brightens creativity and sharpens
insight,
can be obtained
through techniques ranging from
breathing discipline to hypnosis.

These things tone us and tune us to what is
already inside
of our spirits
and sometimes attract a flash, a glimpse, a
brief infusion
from the spirit-light that surrounds us.

But the Holy Spirit is the complete source,
the reliable source,
the true source.

When we *ask* for the Holy Spirit
to guide our growth,
to give us wings of thoughtful awareness,
we connect ourselves directly,
we plug into the source-current
of spiritual serendipity.

The Process
(of Seeking the Gift)

Now, the bold revelation:
This book proposes nothing less than
a new way of planning
and a new way of living.
As suggested earlier,
The new way of living is called "watching."

The new way of planning is called "prayer."
Watch and pray.
These two words are the process, the how.
Watch and pray is the simple (and Biblical)
formula
for serendipity of the spirit.

Time now to unravel the simplicity—
to open up the formula's two elements,
discover their makeup—
so both can be reconstituted
inside our souls.

Higher-realm watching is a physical art,
and a skill of *sense and mind*
that can be enhanced and magnified
by the spirit.
Higher-realm prayer is a spiritual art, and a
skill of *soul*
that can be both directed and answered
by the spirit.
Both of these arts/skills/gifts can be learned,
developed, improved.

The admonition to watch
occurs dozens of times in scriptures
and holy books.
In the New Testament,
it is frequently repeated advice
of Christ and His apostles.

Think of two different but complementing
connotations:
watch *for* and anticipate the good . . . and
watch *out* for the bad.

Scriptures admonish us to watch *unto* prayer.
It is as we watch that we learn to recognize
and "see"
just what it is that we should pray for.
Thus, watching leads us to pray.
And prayer, in turn, leads us to watch
because it brings impressions, insights, ideas
about
what to watch for.
We should watch that we might better pray
and we should pray
that we might better watch.

Prayer, when it is watchful, is thoughtful,
insightful,
and directed to the real needs
that our awareness
has revealed to us.

Watching, when it is prayerful, is transparent,
clear,
and free of the self-conscious filters
of pseudo self-reliance.

But enough theory.
Just how do we perfect the art of true watching?

And how do we develop our sagacity and our
ability
to ponder, to magnify light,
and to marshal our own inner sight so that it
mingles
with the higher sight of prayer?

In approaching the *how*, two preface
caveats . . .
First: How to watch and how to pray are
questions which
require individual answers,
not collective ones.
Directional pointers can be given,
but not a full personal explanation
(a compass rather than a road map).
Second: Since watch and pray
are like chicken and egg
(adroit watching enhances our prayer and
adept prayer enhances our watching),
they need not
(perhaps should not) be approached
sequentially.
They can grow together.

But for discussion . . . prayer first . . .
because it is the power that lifts our watching
above the level of mental serendipity, which
we have
already discussed.

Praying for Guidance
*(Four Suggestions
for Developing the Art)*

When we say "praying for guidance" we could
also say:

Admitting what we don't know
and asking someone who does,
or
Admitting what we can't do
and asking someone who can,
or
Seeking internal and external answers
through thought and prayer,
or
Creating things spiritually
before we create them physically,
or
Developing a superior alternative to
(or an advanced form of) planning,
or
Setting and regularly adjusting goals
in an attempt to match His will,
or
One-half of the formula for spiritual serendipity.

How to improve your prayer? Four suggestions:

1 Hold Regular Sunday Sessions and Set Goals Without Plans

Expand the Sunday-session suggestion
of mental serendipity
to include the spiritual element.
Set aside an hour of Sunday solitude
to review the directions and goals of your life
through thought and prayer.
Think of yourself as a ship
with internal compass and guidance systems
but also able to get bearings from the heavens.
Project in writing where you want to be
and what you want to have "brought to pass"
(in your family, in your work,
in your personal life)
five years from now.

Then check it through prayer against
God's will.
Adjust your goals (or refine them)
from week to week
during this prayerful Sunday session.
Reflect and ponder on how you will get to
these goals
(from where you are now)
but be content with broad-brush pictures
and conceptual images.

Stop short of the detailed, complex plans
that assume you know more
than you really do
and block the way of both inspiration
and discovery.

When I first made a commitment to the idea
of Sunday sessions, I was very disciplined and
rigorous about the process. I even used an an-
tique hourglass to graphically concentrate my
mind on the future (the sand in the top) and to
impose the use of the *whole* hour. My habit was
to carefully and prayerfully review and think
through my longer-range goals, then to decide
on weekly goals that would move me along toward them. I then planned each of the next six
days, in rather exhaustive detail, often hour by
hour, in an attempt to assure myself of reach-
ing the weekly goals.

The results were not altogether satisfactory.
Unanticipated and irritating things came up
every day, and there was often a certain amount
of frustration at the end of the week when all
the goals were not met. Too much planning!
On the other extreme, whenever I missed
holding my Sunday session, the week seemed
aimless and even more frustrating. Too little
planning!

Then one week I had an experience that gave
me some unexpected insight. I had started my
Sunday session, complete with hourglass, and

had reviewed my long-term goals, thoughtfully, prayerfully set some clear objectives for
the coming week, and written them in my little
pocket diary. Just as I was beginning my detailed time plan (*when* and *where* and *how* to do
what), I was interrupted by a small family
emergency and never did make it back to finish
my session. During the week ahead there were
no detailed plans and lists to check off, but I
did glance frequently at the goals.

When the next Sunday came, I grabbed my
trusty hourglass and sat down, determined not
to be deterred this time from my full one-hour
planning regimen. As usual, I started by re-
viewing my goals for the past week. To my surprise, I had met them all. I had done so *without*
detailed time planning or scheduling—almost
subconsciously it seemed.

And as I thought about it, I realized that the
week had been more pleasant than usual—
more natural and somehow slower, easier. It
seemed as if I'd enjoyed myself more, noticed
more, perhaps had more fun. I hadn't felt the
aimlessness that was usually the penalty for
missing a Sunday session; *nor* had I felt the
pressure and the irritation of a lot of little detailed plans that kept getting interrupted or
went unimplemented.

But wait, I'd always been taught—I'd always
taught—that goals weren't much good without
plans: you have to count the cost, you have to

decide the where, when, and how as well as the what!

Then something occurred to me: When we set goals, and pray about them, we receive God's confirmation on *what* we should do. To ask for similar confirmation on the detail of exactly when, where, and how we should do them may be slightly presumptuous and may signify an unwillingness to go some of the distance by faith. We can have some ideas about when, where, and how, but recognizing how little we know, and how much is beyond our control, these ideas should be flexible.

Then something else occurred to me: Having a conceptual picture of how we hope to *use* time to reach worthy goals is one thing, but closely planning and scheduling all of "our" time not only assumes that we know more than we do, it assumes (dangerously) that time really *belongs* to us. Perhaps it is more accurate to think of time as a temporary stewardship that God has given us. Perhaps our objective should be to use it according to His will. We should plan to devote time to goals we have prayerfully set. But we should be committed to *watch* both for unexpected moments and methods to reach these goals and for other, unplanned ways in which He wants us to use His time.

Then a third thing occurred to me: Planning is like aiming. No matter how well you aim,

you may (especially if your target is moving)
miss. But with certain servomechanisms, like
heat-seeking guided missiles or sound-seeking
torpedoes, you just aim in the general direction of the target and the mechanism auto-
matically makes whatever adjustments are
necessary to score a hit. Goals that are well
and prayerfully set are "guided." What we need
is the *thought* to take careful aim, followed by
the *faith* to keep the guidance system working.

God often confirms the *what*
and helps us with our *aim* as we *pray*.
Then, if we are spiritually sagacious,
He refines and adjusts the
where, when, and *how*
(and sometimes even adds to the *what*)
as we *watch*.

2 Develop the Skill and the Habit and the Power of Thoughtful Asking

Ask
is the most repeated admonition in scripture
and is the key that unlocks blessings and
guidance
without violation of our agency.

Think about that.
If God has given us mortality
to progress, to develop, to grow into ourselves,
then we must have agency and options.
And if He intervenes without invitation,
agency is undermined.
But when we ask, it is *our* initiative,
and guidance is answers, not interference.

Because of its power, we must be careful
in our asking.
"Beware of what you want," the saying goes,
"for you will get it."
G. K. Chesterton said,
"By asking for pleasure, we lose the
chief pleasure,
for the chief pleasure is surprise."

But when asking is thoughtful,
and when it follows unselfish
thanking,
it polishes us and pleases our Father
and prayer becomes sweet and delicious
and
hard-to-conclude.
Good askers are good listeners
and willing to watch and wait.

Prayer sometimes yields inspiration about
what *we* can do to answer our own question or
meet our own needs. One praying for a solu-

tion or answer might be spiritually prompted to a place, a person, or a passage that contains the form or formula needed. One praying for material needs or deeper fulfillment might be spiritually directed toward a new field or a different kind of work.

Other times prayer is not the source of an answer or the channel by which we are guided to do something ourselves. Rather, it *is* the answer and brings about the change by itself without directing us to do anything!

Sometimes prayer is the source of power.
Sometimes it *is* the power.
More things are wrought by prayer
than any of us dream. . . .
Lincoln said, "Sometimes I am driven to my knees
by the overwhelming conviction
that I have nowhere else to go."
God, just as a wise earthly father might do,
often prompts us, guides us toward our own answers,
helps us solve our own problems.
And when needs and worthy requests
are far beyond us,
He lifts us beyond ourselves
or gives to us beyond our understanding.

There are at least four very different types of prayer in which God's guidance is sought:

Prayer for *light*, where we seek a clear mind, insight, wisdom, true impressions and direction toward correct decisions and God's will— so that we can decide what to do and then do it.

Prayer for *might*, where we ask for the power to be able to do what we ourselves cannot do.

Prayer for *change* wrought by God, where we ask God to bring to pass things far beyond our own capacity or power.

Prayer for *confirmation* after we have made a decision and are requesting God's approval before we implement it.

3 Learn the Fourth (and Most Forgotten) Type of Prayer

Think further about prayers for confirmation. Acknowledging the short limits of our understanding, we seek confirmation—the still, sure nod that says "yes" to our own careful conclusions, goals, and decisions. At this level, our prayers are true-false rather than multiple choice or open-ended and God's promise

is of a yes (a burning or a calm knowing)
or a no (a stupor of thought).

Confirmation, once received,
is confidence,
assurance and support in hard times . . .
and freedom from
the plague of the second guess.

I learned God's pattern for giving prayer-
answer confirmation on our decisions from a
wise old mentor. I had gone to him for advice
when I realized I was in love and needed to
make the biggest decision of my life—about
marriage.

My wise friend listened, amused, to my love-
sick account of exhilaration mixed with trepi-
dation and asked me if I had prayed.

"Nonstop," I said. "I've thought of nothing
else and I've prayed to know what to do."

"You've left out the middle step," he said.
"First you must ponder and analyze your own
heart and mind—praying for clarity but not for
an easy answer. *Then you make your own decision.*
Then you take that decision to God in prayer
and ask for a spiritual confirmation that it is
right.

"Think about it," he said. "Would a wise father just give you important answers, or would
He encourage you to work out your answers as
best you could and then bring them to him to

be checked or approved?" Then he gave me a challenge. "Fast for a day or two to develop humility and clarity," he said. "Then make your decision, take it to the Lord, and ask Him a single simple question: 'Is my decision *right?*' Ask for validation, for approval, and for the ringing affirmation of the spirit that will allow you never to doubt." He went on, "I promise you that one of two things will happen. Either you'll have a clear, calm feeling of sure confirmation, or you'll have a troubled stupor of thought indicating that you should rethink, that you should go back to the drawing board, that for now at least your decision is not right."

I followed his advice. Making my own decision was not difficult. I simply acknowledged that I was deeply in love with Linda and that my heart and mind had decided to ask Linda to be my wife. Then, fasting, I went to the mountains, knelt in the snow, and asked for confirmation.

After a time, it came softly and peacefully, with *deep* reassurance. A similar confirmation, through a similar process, came to Linda. Since then, through all the thick and thin, all the ups and downs of our marriage, we have never doubted, never second-guessed, never looked back.

A confirmation is a pure, sure yes,
a green light to go ahead,

an assurance from one who knows all
that you who know so little nonetheless have
made a decision that is right.
A divine confirmation is a heart-deposit of
peace,
a sure memory
to fall back on when doubts drop in.

Another time, years later, we applied the
three-step confirmation process to a very different type of decision. I had been offered a
presidential appointment to direct a once-a-
decade White House conference. It dealt with
a worthy subject (children and parents), it was
a clear opportunity, and it would allow us to
spend a year at our "other home" in Washington, D.C. It also seemed to open doors to the
other contributions we hoped to make. Linda
and I analyzed it, talked to the children, and
became collectively excited about a tentative
decision to go.

But in prayer the confirmation didn't come.
We wanted it, we tried for it, we even tried to
imagine that we had felt it. But with spiritual
confirmations, if you're not sure you've felt
them, you haven't.

We discussed it again. We couldn't think of
any negatives other than the inconvenience of
a move back to Washington and the need to
turn parts of our business over to others for a
time.

Then we rationalized a little. Maybe it didn't matter that much to God whether we accepted or declined. Maybe this wasn't a stupor of thought we were getting but rather an "Okay, fine, go ahead if you want to." We went ahead. It was one of those interesting decisions that wasn't really wrong, but it wasn't really right either. Only a few weeks after our return to Washington, President Reagan was shot and the difficulty of his recovery, coupled with other factors, led him to de-emphasize the conference and redirect most of its activity to a state level rather than the national level that I was assigned to direct.

With hindsight we realized that there were ways in which we could have had the same experience without giving up as much as we did. I could have chaired the conference rather than being its director, made a part-time rather than full-time commitment, kept the other parts of my profession going. We had made a decision based on limited foresight and realized now that what had come to us in prayer was a stupor of thought, signaling the need to rethink, to take a different approach.

A stupor of thought is a signal
to start over.
Either the wrong fork has been taken, or
something has been left out, a piece is missing
somewhere.

Or perhaps the timing is wrong.
The stupor is the *absence* of sureness
and is both as real and as valuable
as the confirmation, which is
(unless we give up)
yet to come.

4 Develop the Attitude of "Nothingness"

G. K. Chesterton said,
"It is impossible without humility
to enjoy anything—even pride." He also said,
"If a man would make his world large,
he must make himself small."
Indeed, we cannot fully appreciate God's
greatness
or maximize the power and use of faith
until we understand (or at least acknowledge)
our own nothingness.

God wants us to know both how unlimited
our potential is
and *how far* we have to go to reach it—
so that we can feel both the confidence and
familiarity
of closeness
and the humility and awe of distance.

A great speaker once brought those two, humility and confidence, together in my mind. He spoke of the number of stars that astronomy had discovered (it was some unimaginable number—a seven followed by fifteen zeros as I recall). To illustrate how large the number was he asked us to imagine a book with that number of pages. How thick would the book be? One hundred feet thick? A mile? A hundred miles? "No," he said, "a book with that many pages would circle the world a thousand times." Then he said, "That's how many stars or suns we've located. Each of them has planets circling it, and you are a tiny speck on one of those planets orbiting around one of those stars."

I remember feeling myself grow smaller and smaller and disappear into total insignificance.

Then the speaker concluded with one powerful statement that restored the balance of significance and nothingness. "When I look out upon the heavens," he said, "I see the *handwork* of God. But when I look out on your faces, I see God's *offspring*."

As God's children
we have unlimited potential.
But how important to remember,
always remember,
especially in prayer,
how very far we are from that potential . . .

to *exercise* humility for self and awe for God,
to sense the vastness of the distance between.

"Beware of professed Christians"
said C. S. Lewis
"who possess insufficient awe of Christ."
Neal Maxwell said,
"The more we ponder where we stand in
relation to Christ
the more we realize that
we do not stand at all . . .
we only kneel."
The "attitude of awe"
is an essential part of the recipe
for spiritual serendipity.

Besides asking for light, might, change, and
confirmation, there are two other ways to
feel the calm, aware feelings and the guided
promptings of spiritual serendipity through
prayer. One is to simply *ask for the feeling.* Once
you have felt serendipity of your spirit, recognized it, identified it, desired to have it more,
ask for it in prayer. Focus your faith (mental effort) on how it feels, on why you want it, and
on God's power to give it—and *ask* for it.

Another (less direct but equally effective)
way to ask for spiritual serendipity is to ask *for
opportunities to give service*, for enhanced sensitivity and awareness of others' needs. *Ask* for

promptings of insight or empathy that would allow you to lend a hand, give a compliment, share a burden, ease a pain, be a friend. It is the mirrors of self-awareness and self-preoccupation that close us in—and block out the broader awareness that triggers serendipity. The clear windows of bright perception open when we look for the needs of others and ask for opportunities to serve. With the noticing of needs comes the insight of ideas, the receiving of relationships, and the observation of opportunities of all kinds.

And the feeling of peace, worth, and light that comes from the smallest act of giving or serving is so similar to the feeling of spiritual serendipity that it must *be* spiritual serendipity.

Can we further define and understand serendipity by putting it up against its opposite? The antonym of serendipity is *selfishness*. A preoccupation with *my* needs, *my* goals, *my* problems, and *my* point of view relegates us to the dark tunnel of predictable prejudices and the dungeon of self, shutting out the sky of other possibilities, other people, and the endless space and freedom of serendipity.

Watching for Guidance
*(Four Suggestions
for Developing the Art)*

When we say, "watching for guidance," we
could also say:

Perceiving the answers that are already there,
or
Seeing through windows
instead of into mirrors,
or
Taking off our blinders,
or
Seeing with ears and hearts as well as eyes,
or
Noticing what's going on inside
and outside ourselves,
or
Feeling when to act,
and acting on what you feel,
or
Looking for God's will in all situations,
or
The other half of the formula for
spiritual serendipity.

How to improve your watching? Four
suggestions:

1 Add to the Attitude (of Sagacity)

Mental serendipity requires sagacity
and an attitude of calm, interested watching.
Spiritual serendipity requires the addition of a
higher
and deeper watching
through a still, observant soul, and
through the inner eye of the spirit.
For this higher realm, we need an open heart
and the kind of wise watching
wherein we not only try to see the little things
but try to see them *as answers.*

Once we have asked we must watch for
unexpected answers
in unexpected forms.
Answers are sometime found in silver linings,
and other times in the clouds themselves.

Taking off on a business flight one evening,
we flew west, up into a heavy cloud bank and
toward the sunset. The deep gray was haloed
by gold and the metaphor of "silver linings"
passed through my mind. We entered the
cloud and experienced some bouncing and buf-
feting. Then we burst through it directly in-

to the yellow brilliance of the setting sun—high
enough now that the sun had come back up. It's
interesting, I thought, that the clouds which
often dominate our vision are only vapors—
while the silver lining is the reality of the sun.

The attitude that spurs spiritual serendipity
not only causes us to look for silver linings,
but helps us understand that,
despite appearances,
they are vaster and stronger by far
than the clouds in front of them,
and are provided by the same source
and force.
Ask as though everything depended on God
(because it does).
Watch as though everything depended on
you
(because the answer may be right in front
or right inside of you).
Do not limit your watching or looking
to your solutions, your answers,
your interests.
Look wider. See 360 degrees.
By looking away, we see deeper inside.
And by seeing the needs of others,
we find answers for ourselves.

2 Add Gratitude
to Attitude
(and Also Fasting)

Why would gratitude help us to watch?
Because gratitude is awareness of blessings!
The same perceptive inner sight that reveals
gratitude
for what *has* happened
also reveals answers and guidance
in what *is* happening.

Thankfulness is perfect training for
watchfulness.
One who sees the past's blessings
sees also the present's answers
and the future's opportunities.

Fasting, going without food for a day
to cleanse and purge the body,
also opens and tunes the mind and spirit.
Anciently it was a principle often used
in connection with asking
for blessings,
but it can also assist in giving thanks
for blessings.
When we fast with thanksgiving
and joyful hearts,

"fasting" can become a synonym for
"rejoicing."
It can sharpen our physical senses
and tune in our spiritual senses, making us
highly
susceptible
to spiritual serendipity.

Many years ago, we started a Thanksgiving
tradition in our family of listing our blessings.
Before we sit down to eat the turkey dinner, we
make a list on a long roll of cash register paper
of every blessing we can think of. Everyone in
the family gets involved and we list everything
from "a free country" to "indoor plumbing."

After dinner, we have contests to see who can
read the entire list in the shortest amount of
time.

Each time we practice this tradition, we realize that gratitude is more than something we
owe to God. It is a beautiful *feeling*. It is something we should summon and savor as a gift to
ourselves.

"Gratitude."
A trivialized word, or at least undervalued.
We say "thanks"—or feel a fleeting wave
of appreciation—just a thin skin
covering over our take-for-granted
mantra mentality.

Instead, gratitude can be a joyful awakening to
God's glory,
to our own happily dependent childhood,
our ultimate-potential nothingness,
a powerful spiritual emotion,
thrilling us to our core, tearing our eye,
striking deep-space awe
and humility so pure it hurts.

Without humility we develop a
preposterous paradigm
of world-shrinking, self-bloating arrogance
or imagined self-sufficiency.
Humility has only two approaches:
crisis or gratitude.
And scripture calls "more blessed"
those who are
"humble without being compelled
to be humble" (approach two).

Not some luxury, then, gratitude,
not some diversion to indulge in
occasionally,
not mere etiquette or brief warmth-flashes.
But a way of life, a profound gift/skill
(itself worthy of high thanks)
involving seeing, feeling, sharing, and
abundant love,
Yielding humility, perspective, peace, and
abundant joy.

3 Respond to
(and Remember)
Spiritual Promptings

When a "nudge" or impression touches our
spirit
(sometimes just brushing gently across it)
the worst thing we can do is to ignore it.
The second worst thing we can do
is to forget it.
These impressions often reach clarity only for
an instant and then
begin to fade, dim and dissipate . . .
unless we seize them and transfer them
into our conscious mind,
where they can be held solid and clear.

So many experiences of failure illustrate this
need to tune in. I think of the time when
we moved to England for a year. We had three
teenagers—all of whom got incredibly home-
sick, one in particular.

Just a week after we arrived, and *before*
homesickness began, I was running an errand
with our fifteen-year-old and felt a clear
"nudge" to talk with her about the homesickness that would probably set in after the excitement wore off. It was clear to me for a moment
just how to explain certain things—just what to

say to prepare her and soften the blow. Just then we got to where we were going so I decided to wait and discuss it later.

A half hour later, on the way home, I brought up the concept of homesickness, but the clear insight into how to explain it and prepare her for it was gone.

Several days later, when the symptoms had arrived in force, we talked again (I talked, she *sobbed*) and I was able to explain some of what I should have explained earlier. As I did, I realized how much more good it would have done if I had followed the first nudge when it came.

Learn to recognize impressions that come
from the spirit,
and categorize them not with imagination,
superstition,
or chance
but with inspiration and light.

Focus on nudges or impressions or little
flashes of insight
and *remember* them.
If possible, act on them immediately.
(I've decided that the best reason to have a
cellular phone
is that you usually *reach* people
if you call them the minute you feel the
nudge.)

If you can't act immediately on impressions,
capture them by writing them down.
As you write, they will expand and become
more clear.
Writing can be thought of as the "tuning in"
that makes a faint signal
audible and understandable.

4 Use Split-Page
Planning with
"Nudge Notes"

When a spiritual impression comes,
it may not be something you can act on
immediately but
something you should do at some particular
future time . . .
or it may be someone you should see,
or something you should say.
The best place to make notes on these nudges
is in your planner or date book,
so that you commit yourself to a specific time
on a particular day.

Other impressions may come in the form of
broader, longer-range ideas
that can be implemented over time,
or they may come in the form of new insights

that have no particular
or immediate application
but bear remembering.
These longer-range impressions also need to
be captured
in writing.
When they are not written down, they are
loose
and somehow "soluble" . . . they dissolve and
disappear.

I once experienced a particularly forceful lesson on taking seriously and accepting the reality of spiritual impressions. As a young man I
had taken a little time off from college and was
doing a period of volunteer and humanitarian
service in an inner-city ghetto. Another volunteer and I lived together in a small apartment
in a high-rise building. Our supervisor, an en-
ergetic older gentleman, lived on the next floor
with his wife. We called him Elder.

One night late, there was a knock at our
door. It was Elder in a long nightshirt who
said, "My wife is traveling this week so I'm
alone. Could I join you two for evening
prayer?" We invited him in and he suggested
that we kneel down and that I say the prayer. A
little nervous and anxious to impress him, I
went on and on with quite a long prayer, not
wanting to leave anything out.

At one point in the prayer I paused and, with

my head bowed and my eyes closed, I heard the unmistakable sound of a pencil writing on paper. Not wanting to glance up, my first thought was that my roommate, bored with my long prayer and unaware of the importance of our visitor, was starting his nightly letter to his girlfriend.

When I finally finished and looked up, I was shocked to see that it was Elder who had been writing. He had a yellow pad, which was now covered with his long-hand scrawl. He got up, walked to the door, thanked us for letting him join us, and turned to go.

Then he turned back, a twinkle in his eye, and said, "You're probably wondering what I was writing down during the prayer. Simple, really. My memory isn't what it used to be, and when I pray I often get answers, or at least impressions about things I should do. I find that if I don't take notes I tend to forget some of them." With that, he was gone. I remember lying awake that night, thinking, "Prayer is *real* to him. God is real to him. Elder asks, he listens, he takes notes."

Whether nudges come during prayer or meditation or just as we go along living life, it is important to value them, to take them seriously, to remember them, and to act on them. Both short- and long-range nudges can best be recorded with split-page planning described on page 124. Impressions that dictate action can be committed to by an entry on a particu-

lar day ("scheduled" on the left-hand side).
Broader ideas and insights from the same
source can be captured (and expanded) in the
form of notes on the right-hand side. Whatever kind of date book you use can be turned
into a split-page "anti-planner"* by the simple
addition of a vertical line to divide each day.
During Sunday sessions, have a flip-through
review of the week just passed. Pay special attention to any "nudge notes" on the right-hand
side of each day. Think about how they can be
implemented in the future.

Keep Track of Serendipity

As I finish the last pages of this book I am sitting
on a Sri Lanka beach watching men bathe their
elephants and women wash their clothes in the
sea. In my hand is my anti-planner, where I
write my goals and record impressions.

My plans and notes are a little different here
than they would be back in my normal world of
home and office. But the principles are the
same. As I flip back through my split-page
days, I find some Sunday-session goals on the
left-hand side of various pages—things like

---

*So named because, unlike most planners, it helps you be-
come oriented to relationships rather than to achievements and to unplanned serendipity rather than planned
schedules. (See the last page of this book for information
on how to obtain anti-planners.)

"Finish writing Chapter 4" or "Review materials for scuba diving certification test." Also on the left side I see reminders to myself about appointments: "Meet Mr. Ilias at gem factory," "Call Nihal about taxi," "9:05—Flight 515 Air Lanka." Also on the left side I see where I recorded nudges or impressions that I felt I could act on at specific times: "Call long distance to office—get note off to Boyson," "Visit the Bureau of Child Care and Adoption."

But as I look back through the planner pages, I find (as I always do) that the greater value is on the right-hand (serendipity) side of the pages. Here are names and notes about people I met unexpectedly, ideas and feelings I had on subjects ranging from new books to how to get my thirteen-year-old to clean his room, promptings and impressions about things I ought to do and people I ought to call when I get back, and notes on beautiful moments experienced. Whereas the entries on the left-hand side are in the future tense (goals, appointments, etc.), the things on the right are past tense—serendipitous things recorded after the fact. Things like: "Found Henry and the outrigger at Bentara Lagoon," "Had feeling that I should find original Persian fable on Serendip to start book," "Met Tim and Sue at shipping counter," "Followed huge sea turtle while diving," "Impression to spend more time helping Josh with history homework when we return," "Nudge to call publisher and get book distribution in England," "Found Sri Lankan musical instrument store," "Gorgeous sunset across Indian Ocean."

Each entry on the right-hand side brings back a clear memory of a person, a beautiful moment, or a feeling or impression that rang clear and true and needs to be remembered and acted upon. These impressions become a key input on future Sunday sessions as goals are set and time is scheduled.

The entries during our time in Sri Lanka are different from those of normal days at home in normal pursuits. But they are no less exciting or important, because no matter where you are, serendipity removes ruts from life and *converts* routine into surprise and excitement.

How easy it is to slip into life's ruts,
to let routine and rigidity rush and ruin
our days.
Blind routine is ice,
stiff, unflowing and unfeeling,
sitting on the surface of life,
But warm rays of spiritual serendipity can
melt the ice,
letting it flow into and around life's bumpy
topography,
touching the beauty and the pain,
welling up and surging through both sadness
and joy.

Sometimes serendipity even evaporates the ice,
lifting life toward higher, purer feelings and
letting us glimpse the higher realm.

If we want to transform our life's ice
into geysers of water and steam,
we need to warm it, steady and slow, in the glow
of spiritual serendipity.

A Truer Overview
from the Truest Book

This book has tried, through words and
images,
to suggest the formula or recipe
for calmness,
for watching,
for sagacity, and for peaceful, thoughtful
prayer.
But there is a far better statement
of the necessary ingredients of spiritual
serendipity,
far more beautiful,
far more clear, filled with perfect images and
feelings.

The best way you could finish this book
is to set it aside
and read instead from The Book.

Jesus' Sermon on the Mount, recorded in the book of Matthew, has an almost infinite number of messages and light-giving interpretations. One such message, one way to read and interpret the sermon is as an explanation and set of directions of and for spiritual serendipity. Here, read, and feel some of its paraphrased messages and see how they point us toward the attitudes this book has tried to describe:

1. Build your house on a rock—seek treasures in heaven.
   Build your life
   on strong, righteous goals,
   but once they are set . . .
2. Take less thought for the morrow—don't try to plan
   everything.
   Be more like the lilies
   of the field, the birds of the air—
   spontaneous, sensitive, flexible.
3. The light of the body is the eye—see and watch
   and be filled with light—
   ye are the light of the world!
4. Ask, knock, and answers will open.
   Look for those answers and accept them,
   even if they come in unexpected forms.
5. Do not anger or lust—control the mind
   and think purely and deeply.

6. Turn your other cheek—give your cloak—
   love enemies.
7. Instead of judging, strive to *see*
   and understand.
8. Fast in secret, pray in the closet, let not
   the left hand
   see what the right hand gives—have pure,
   inner motives.
9. Rejoice—even in adversity—
   relish and welcome surprises
   and unexpected turns of all kinds.
10. Don't let salt lose its savor—
    don't let life get boring—
    keep your freshness
    and spontaneity.
11. Be perfect—or at least develop the
    perfect attitude
    of receptivity, acceptance, awareness and
    peace;
    record and remember and implement
    every prompting that the
    Spirit gives.

Perhaps it is through something like spiritual serendipity that the meek inherit the earth, and that the humble in spirit *see* the kingdom of God. Read the greatest Sermon again, directly from its source in Matthew's fifth, sixth, and seventh chapters. Read it as a recipe for spiritual serendipity and rediscover its peaceful wisdom.

Curtain Call

Dusk:
sitting on the front veranda of the 130-year-old
Empire Colonial Galle Face Hotel
in Sri Lanka's capital—Colombo.
Looking north where the grassy expanse
called Galle Green
(filled with kites, brass bands, and watchers)
spreads parallel to the sea.
Our plane leaves late tonight—Air Lanka 515
to London.

This land of Serendipity allows you
to take as much of its name home with you as
you wish,
for free
(the minute it was not free it would not be
serendipity).

I came with the goal of
teaching by writing,
but how often I've paused to
learn by watching.
I've decided
that when we look hard enough

for serendipity
and believe in it,
we get a new sense of what's important
(even a new value system)
as a bonus.

I'll bring this book with me
when I leave Serendip tonight,
finished.
But I know now
that there must be two more books.
A spiritual trilogy.
Because I've realized
(here, even as I wrote)
that there are
three
prevalent, popular, pursued, applauded
desires which
diminish our spirituality,
dilute our joy,
divide our faith:
The desire for *control*,
the desire for *ownership*,
the desire for *independence*—
their prickly, rigid, self-directedness
works against the softer flow of the spirit.
Their walls block the bridges;
their mirrors obscure the windows.

We should seek the guidance of serendipity
rather than the tyranny of control,

the freedom of stewardship
rather than the bondage of ownership,
the linkage of synergy
rather than the isolation of independence.

Do you see the need for book II and book III?
We live in an age when it is common and even
popular to seek spirituality, yet we cling to
three perceptions and paradigms that are spirituality's antidotes. Control is fine as an element
of self-discipline; ownership is great as an eco-
nomic principle; independence is important as
a part of personal responsibility.

But as pervasive *attitudes*, each becomes
dulling, manipulative, isolating, and drains
away the power and energy of connected, in-
terdependent spirituality.

We seek to *control* everything when real spirituality is lodged in letting the spirit control
us—in noticing the beauty and opportunity of
circumstance, in finding good currents instead
of swimming upstream, in seeking and accepting *guidance* from our ideas, our impressions, and our insights—in becoming sagacious
enough to find the joy of spontaneity and inspiration, the adventure of the unexpected, the
attitude of *spiritual serendipity*.

We seek *ownership* (which, as a paradigm, always brings with it envy and jealousy or conceit
and pride) when true spirituality is obtained
from understanding that we own nothing and

God owns all, from seeking, instead, treasures of heaven, from adopting the attitude of *spiritual stewardship*.

We seek extreme forms of independence, when real spirituality is logged in dependence on God and on His spirit, in learning from, magnifying, and combining with other people, in operating from the attitude of *spiritual synergy*.

The best alternative attitude to control
is
spiritual serendipity.
The best replacement paradigm for ownership
is
spiritual stewardship.
The best adjusted approach for independence
is
spiritual synergy.

One down, two to go.

a f t e r w o r d

Applications
and Promises

This book wants to end
as it began—with promises.
Hopefully we have made a circle that captures
the ideas necessary
to make the promises look more accessible in
the Afterword
than they did in the Foreword.
Recall the promises back on pages 41–42
and,
based on the pages between there and here,
think for a moment about the *applications*
of spiritual serendipity—
about the benefits that come from being
watchful and prayerful
and using the resulting calm, receptive
serendipity
in each facet of our lives.

1 In Our Work

Spiritual serendipity relaxes us, reduces stress;
helps us find adventure in the day-to-day
possibilities
and opportunity in the small unexpected,
lets us start seeing creative solutions and
cultivating ideas
and lateral-thinking approaches.
Even if your work is, by nature, very routine,
spiritual serendipity will allow you to see and
appreciate
small things about
people and ideas and beauty and situations.
We should realize that serendipity and routine
are mutually exclusive.
Then we should choose serendipity.

I once had a business associate who wrote me
a letter containing his philosophy: "Try never
to be surprised. If you are surprised, it shows
you're not a very good anticipator or planner
and your business life will be unpredictable and
constantly upsetting. Act, don't react, because
we're all judged by what *we* make happen. Learn
to control the people and things around you."

I recently sent him an alternative approach

with parallel wording: "Try to find surprises every day. If you're never surprised it shows you're not a very good watcher and your business life will be dull and consistently boring. Learn to respond as well as to act, because the very measure of our mortality is how we respond to the things that happen to us. Learn to control yourself."

It is possible to go to work with two minds:
One is for making the list, the quota, the deadline, the deal.
The other for noticing the needs,
the opportunities,
the beauty and the humor.
We can write the first, in future tense,
on the left
and write the second, in past tense, on the right.

We can live both sides,
blend them, balance them, be them both.
In addition to our goals and mission statements,
we can learn to rely on nudges, impressions, and
the spiritual sixth sense
to deal with the ongoing questions of work,
to know what, when, where, and how . . .
to succeed both at getting and at giving.
To our ability to work and plan
we can add our ability to watch and pray.

2 In Our Families

Spiritual serendipity helps us see our spouses
and children
more clearly and more individually
so we can spot their needs and
share their joys.

Children are not lumps of clay and we are not
sculptors.
Children are seedlings and we are gardeners.
Each seedling is unique,
needing a particular kind of
watering, nurturing, cultivating.
Our job is not to change their species
but to make them the best of what each
already is.
We know by watching.
Spiritual serendipity also helps us keep
the essential element and energy of humor
in our families and relationships,
and the excitement of flexibility and fun . . .
and it reminds us that our priorities are our
children,
not our plans.

I recall one evening when the "plan" was an
early dinner to allow time for a family activity

before the younger children's bedtime. But the junior high boy was late getting home because he'd had to start over on his crafts project at school which was due tomorrow. It would have been easy to get mad at him except for his look of excitement and pride. He'd learned to use the band saw. He'd discovered a new interest, a new skill. It had been so exciting to him that he'd cut his piece of wood after making only one quick measurement, ruined his project, and had to start over. On his second try everything worked out fine, except that redoing the project made him two hours late getting home. Our late dinner was spent in a discussion that applied the principle of "measure twice, build once" to many different aspects of life. Then since it was late, we all went for ice cream in our pajamas. Nothing went as planned, yet everything turned out *better*.

In a world where the most common
parenting methods
are manipulation
and where we too often push our kids
to become extensions of our own egos,
it is such a relief to adopt a parenting attitude
that is based more on watching
than on winning,
more on feeling than on fighting,
and more on "consulting" and communicating

than on controlling and coercing.
We can draw on a higher power for the higher challenge
of raising children.
We, their finite parents, can ask for help
from their infinite parent.
And with spouse or partner
the surprise and spontaneity
we once called courtship
can now be called marriage serendipity.

3
In Giving Service in the Community or the Church

Spiritual serendipity makes us more
people-oriented,
more *aware* of feelings, needs, opportunities.
This empathy makes service meaningful
rather than mechanical.
God, who knows the needs of all men,
can reveal some of them to you,
and allow you the joy of being His instrument
in meeting them.

"What do you pray for each day?" I remember the question from a teacher of a particu-

larly memorable Sunday school class. She got some standard answers: for safety, for health, for friends and family.

Then she intrigued us all by saying that there was one thing that we would receive every time we prayed for it . . . and that the answers would give us a new level of interest and joy in life.

She let our anticipation build for a moment and then told us that the "always answered" prayer was for opportunities to help or serve others. "Ask for that," she said, "and then *watch*. God will put opportunities in front of you and in each one you will both give joy to someone and find joy for yourself."

The quality of other-awareness and empathy
is both the precipitator and the result of
serendipity.
Service is an exercise in empathy,
and empathy is another word
for the awareness that opens up
channels of inspiration about who needs what
and provides
a million entry points for serendipity.

4 In Leisure and Play

With spiritual serendipity
there is always something to do
even when there's nothing to do.
We see more possibilities, challenges, options,
feel more interests and emotions,
and live longer in the same amount of time.

I remember one particularly beautiful spring day—sunny, bright, beautiful in every way until I looked at the calendar: April 15—income tax day. But, still, I remember thinking, "If I can finish this tax return during the day we can get out and do something relaxing this evening."

But what a day, what a fresh, steady breeze, and what an idea from the six- and eight-year-olds who see kite flying as the ultimate fun.

Figures can be written and subtracted and added after dark, but kites can't be flown. What a day, what a sight to watch the children's eyes dance like their kites, and what a warm memory to carry me through the dark late hours of figuring income tax. (And how lucky that the post office stays open until midnight.)

When asked why we vacation, play, recreate,
we say, "To release, to unwind, to relax."
The same answers could be used
for the question,
"Why serendipity?"
Serendipity is peaceful awareness
and enlightened insights.
Through it, we can
maximize the pleasure and renewal that
leisure is for.

There are a lot of applications
of spiritual serendipity,
a lot of reasons for wanting the quality,
but the reasons all telescope, umbrella, and
fold down
into one word and one reason:
The word is *joy*
and the reason is *progress*
and serendipity is the discovered path
winding along the unending, ever-climbing
ridge
that leads to both.

a s s i s t a n c e

Some people come to the end
of a book they've come to believe in
and ask
"How?"
They say "Thanks for the textbook
but where is the workbook?"
As it turns out, there is a workbook
for spiritual serendipity
in the form of a larger book and an audio
seminar,
both called *Lifebalance*.

It took me and Linda twenty years of writing
to reach the conclusion that what we really
wanted to say (and what we really wanted
to have) was *balance:* Balance between work,
family, and personal needs; balance between
structure and spontaneity, balance between relationships and achievements. We tried to understand and explain all three kinds of balance
in the book *Lifebalance*, published by Simon &
Schuster.

That book is very much about serendipity,
but very little about spiritual serendipity. This
book can be thought of as the spiritual supple-

ment to that one (or that can be thought of as the secular supplement to this one).

Lifebalance, however, comes with some things that this book doesn't. It has step-by-step *methods* and suggests life-pattern-changing *habits*. And it "fits together" with an eight-session Lifebalance seminar (each session consisting of an audio tape, a workbook, and a set of "anti-planners," which *teach* the steps involved in obtaining balance and developing serendipity).

One final thought: I've tried to make this a spiritual book but not a religious one. I felt this was important because the principles of spiritual serendipity are true (and usable) for people of any religion—or of no religion. Still, there are those who inquire about my own personal religious beliefs. For them I have written a book called *The Wrappings and the Gifts*. It is available by calling either of the numbers below:

- To ask questions about any aspect of serendipity, lifebalance, or the author's broader beliefs . . . or about membership in HOMEBASE, an international organization of over 100,000 parents who work cooperatively to implement the ideas and directions suggested by the Eyres' books, call (801) 581-0112.
- To simply order books, anti-planners, or the eight-part Lifebalance seminar, call (800) 772-4859.

i n d e x